THE
HORTI
S
HAN

The official RHS guide to organising, judging and competing in a show

For the guidance of organisers,
schedule-makers, exhibitors and judges

Revised 2008

The Royal Horticultural Society

Published by
The Royal Horticultural Society
80 Vincent Square, London SW1P 2PE, United Kingdom
www.rhs.org.uk

Copyright © The Royal Horticultural Society
1953, 1956, 1972, 1981, 1990, 1999, 2008
First published 1953
Seventh edition 2008
ISBN 9781902896830

Printed and bound in the UK by Page Bros, Norwich

Cover design: Simon Garbutt

Photographs Front cover: Liz Eddison
Back cover (top to bottom) *left column:* Liz Eddison, Tim Sandall,
Liz Eddison, Tim Sandall; *centre column:* Tim Sandall, Liz Eddison,
Tim Sandall; *right column:* Liz Eddison, Tim Sandall, Liz Eddison.

• Further copies of this book are available at RHS Gardens
and from RHS Mail Order: tel 0845 260 4505;
email mailorder@rhs.org.uk; online www.rhs.org.uk

CONTENTS

SHOW STATIONERY

Items of show stationery are available to societies that are members of the Affiliated Societies scheme run by the RHS.

For all stationery queries and information on prices and ordering, please contact:

**RHS Enterprises Limited, Mail Order Department, RHS Garden Wisley, Woking, Surrey, GU23 6QB
Tel: 0845 260 4505
Email: mailorder@rhs.org.uk**

RHS AFFILIATED SOCIETY MEMBERSHIP

The Affiliated Societies membership scheme is open to gardening clubs and societies with a remit to promote horticulture at a local level. A valuable package of benefits is provided.

For further information please contact:

**Affiliated Societies, RHS, 80 Vincent Square, London SW1P 2PE
Tel. 020 7821 3069
Email: affsocs@rhs.org.uk**

PREFACE TO THE 2008 (7TH) EDITION

The first edition of *The Horticultural Show Handbook*, published in 1953, was an important landmark in the process of establishing and rationalising rules and regulations governing the exhibition of flowers, fruits and vegetables at horticultural shows. The guidance offered in the 1953 edition and subsequently updated in 1956, 1972, 1981, 1990 and 1999, has been widely accepted by organisers of horticultural shows, exhibitors and judges throughout the UK, and this small book has become the standard reference for all those who organise or take part in events at every level.

The 2008 edition has been updated in full consultation with specialist societies, RHS Committees, and other experts. Of particular note is the fact that the *Handbook* now complements guidelines published by the National Vegetable Society and the Royal National Rose Society.

A new introductory section has been added – *How to Stage a Local Flower Show* – which aims to offer guidance and advice to those who have never before organised a show. In addition, generic guidelines for judging vegetables have been introduced in an effort to cover the many exotic and unusual cultivars that are increasingly found at local shows. "Advice to judges" comments have been included for all vegetables, some fruit and some flowers.

Throughout their work, the experts involved in developing this edition have endeavoured to make the book more user-friendly and relevant to small, amateur shows as they realise only too well that these are the breeding grounds for future award winners at major RHS events. Particular effort has been made to encourage show secretaries, judges and schedulers to do their utmost to include classes that will accommodate all levels of exhibitor and to assist those new to showing in every way. With this publication, the Society hopes to inspire keen gardeners of all ages and levels of experience to enjoy and continue the tradition of exhibiting at horticultural shows.

January 2008

Inga Grimsey
Director General

ACKNOWLEDGEMENTS

The Society is most grateful to the many people who have contributed to the revision. In particular it wishes to thank Mr Colin Spires who has given unstintingly of his time and expertise in chairing many meetings of the Working Groups who undertook this latest revision. Members of the various Working Groups who gave freely of their time and experience to dissect, re-assemble and check the text to ensure its accuracy are the following members of the National Vegetable Society, the RHS Fruit Group and various RHS Floral and Plant Trials Committees: Mr Jim Arbury, Mr Harry Baker, Mr Peter Collett, Dr P R Dawson, Mr Gerald Edwards, Mr Malcolm Evans and Mr Medwyn Williams MBE. All have been enormously helpful in giving generously of their expertise in the revision but special thanks are due to Mr Malcolm Evans who was particularly instrumental in carrying through the changes to *The Judging of Vegetables* section, and to Mrs Anita Foy who acted as secretary to the various working groups and who worked tirelessly on the many revisions.

The Society also wishes to acknowledge the help of the numerous Specialist Societies, show judges and individuals who provided detailed comments and advice on sections applicable to their own discipline.

• Any suggestions for amendments to *The Horticultural Show Handbook* are welcomed and should be sent to:

> **RHS Gardening Advice Service,**
> **80 Vincent Square,**
> **London SW1P 2PE**

HOW TO STAGE A LOCAL FLOWER SHOW

It can be a very satisfying experience to be involved in the running of a local flower show. The points below are intended to give some basic guidance to those new to staging shows.

The list is not exhaustive but used alongside other relevant sections of this *Handbook* should provide guidance to anyone organising a flower show for the first time.

1 Timing and venue   It is first necessary to consider the timing of the show, potential clashes with local events, the cropping season in the district and to write the schedule to include the flowers, fruit and vegetables that are likely to be available at the time the show is to be held. The date needs to be fixed long in advance and the judges appointed early. Visit other flower shows to get ideas and information.

A suitable venue needs to be booked – with plenty of light, large enough for the anticipated number of exhibits (but not too large), and with running water. Other matters to organise are the provision of tabling, vases, plates, etc.

2 What is the level of the exhibitor who is likely to compete?   Consider whether you wish to include classes for flower arrangement (judged under NAFAS rules), domestic produce, novices and children's classes. Consider also whether novelty classes (such as heaviest marrow, pumpkin, onion, etc) may be appropriate.

3 What awards are to be given?   If your society/show is affiliated to the RHS, an RHS Bronze medal can be purchased from the RHS, as can a Banksian Medal (which can only be awarded to the exhibitor who received the most prize money at the show, the winners in the previous two years being ineligible.) Other national specialist societies (such as the Daffodil Society, the National Vegetable Society, the National Dahlia Society, the National Chrysanthemum Society, the British Fuchsia Society and the Royal National Rose Society) offer medals in their own specialist sections to affiliated shows.

4 Prepare the show schedule well in advance If preparing a schedule for the first time, seek advice from those familiar with organising shows of a similar type, or contact the RHS. Decide on entry fees, prize money and awards.

Do not seek too many specimens per class. Remember that the quantities suggested in this *Handbook* are for county or national shows.

The rules of the show must be made clear. It is recommended that the rules are stated in the schedule. The Royal Horticultural Society's rules *(see pp10–12)* are suitable for most shows, with additions as appropriate.

Arrange for the entries to be taken by as many people as practicable.

Make sure that the schedule is available to exhibitors and judges as far before the show as possible. *(See also pp21–28, Suggestions to Schedule Makers.)*

5 The wording of classes *(See also pp26–28, Paragraphs 27 and 28)* Make classes clear and simple to understand. If, for example, a rule is incorporated as follows: "unless otherwise stated, each exhibit must be staged in one vase (or dish as appropriate) and must consist of one cultivar only", then classes can read as follows: (a) Daffodils, division 1, 3 blooms, (b) Dahlias, medium decorative, 3 blooms, (c) Tomatoes, medium, 5, or (d) Dessert apples, 4.

Alternatively, if mixed cultivars of flowers are to be allowed, the above classes should read: (a) Daffodils, division 1, 3 blooms, 1 or more cultivars, or (b) Dahlias, medium decorative, 3 blooms, 1 or more cultivars.

• **Note:** Mixed cultivars are not allowed in single dishes in fruit and vegetable classes.

6 Tabling Traditionally, show tables are placed in lines with the first row along a wall. This is the most efficient use of space. At large shows, tiered staging is sometimes used and this can add to the visual effect. Sometimes the show room is rather larger than is ideal, and in such cases some show organisers have successfully used circular tables, suitably placed, which allows more space for visitors to view the exhibits.

It is important to give thought to tabling space for each class, as the space required will vary from class to class. As a general guide, a dish of fruit will require 30cm of table width, as would a container of a single cut flower. While up to three dishes of fruit can be staged directly behind each other, more space should be allowed for flowers, in order that all exhibits can be seen. For example, a class of single flower with three entries could take 45cm of table width. It is difficult to give advice on pot-plant classes, as the size of plants will vary considerably. Show organisers have the right to move exhibits if space becomes too crowded. In extreme cases, it may be more practical to move a class entirely to another staging area. In such cases, organisers should remember to advise the judges.

7 On the day   Ensure there is an area where exhibitors can stage their exhibits. Allow plenty of space, as some exhibitors like to spread out.

Make sure that there are enough helpers and judges' stewards.

RULES

Unless otherwise stated in the schedule, the following rules apply to all competitions held by the Royal Horticultural Society.

These rules are suitable for incorporation in the schedules of many local horticultural societies if 'the Committee' is substituted for 'the Society'.

1 Acceptance of entries   The Society reserves the right to refuse any entry and, in the event of such refusal, it is not required to give any reason or explanation.

2 Eligibility of exhibitors   On all questions regarding the eligibility of an exhibitor the decision of the relevant committee of the Society shall be final.

3 Exhibits must be the property of the exhibitor   Unless the Show Schedule specifically states otherwise, any plant, flower, fruit or vegetable exhibited in competition must be the property of the person in whose name it is entered, and must have been grown from seed by the exhibitor or been in his/her possession or cared for by him/her for at least two months prior to the date of the show. In the case of a professional gardener entering produce from the garden in which he/she is employed the exhibits must be entered in the name of the employer.

4 Number of entries per household   Unless otherwise stated in the schedule, two or more persons may not compete separately in the same class with produce from the same garden and/or allotment. If members of a household wish to share the credit and prizes then the exhibits should be entered in joint names. This ruling does not apply to classes such as floral arrangement where exhibitors are allowed to use plant material that has not been grown by themselves.

5 Constitution of an exhibit   Where a number or quantity of plants, flowers, fruit or vegetables is specified in the schedule for a class, vase, dish or collection, neither more nor less than the number or quantity may be shown and an exhibit will be disqualified for any excess or deficiency.

If, before an exhibit is judged, any excess or deficiency is noticed and considered to be the result of an accident and not of an attempt to deceive, the referee, steward or secretary may either give the exhibitor (if at hand) an opportunity to correct the mistake or correct it himself/ herself but the officials shall not be under any obligation to do so and any disqualification resulting from an excess or deficiency shall be the exhibitor's responsibility. The judges may not correct any error but they may direct the attention of the referee, steward or secretary to it.

6 The naming of exhibits   All exhibits should be correctly named. Errors in naming will not disqualify the entry but the judges should regard correctness and clearness of naming as telling in favour of an exhibit in a close competition.

If the exhibitor does not know the name of any cultivar the label should bear the words "name unknown".

When an unnamed seedling is shown (*eg* a seedling daffodil) the label should bear the word "seedling", and may be followed by an indicative number.

7 Constitution of dishes   Every dish must consist of one cultivar (variety) only, unless mixed dishes are permitted by the schedule.

8 Quantities   The quantities specified in *The Judging of Fruits* and *The Judging of Vegetables (see p49 and pp70–72)* are those used for RHS and leading provincial shows. Individual schedule-makers may wish to reduce these quantities to suit the size and scope of their own shows.

8 Only one prize in a class   No exhibitor may be awarded more than one prize in any one class unless that is specifically permitted by the schedule. *(See also p18, paragraph 12.)*

9 Prizes may be withheld   Any prize may be withheld or modified if the exhibits are considered unworthy of the prize offered.

10 Exhibits not according to schedule   Any exhibit that does not conform to the wording of the schedule (unless corrected in accordance with Rule 5) must be disqualified and a judge must write on the entry card "Not according to schedule" (NAS) and add a factual note as to why it is marked NAS. Single dishes in an NAS collection cannot be considered for any other award.

11 Decisions   The decision of the judges shall be final on the relative merits of the exhibits, but the Society reserves the right to refer any points in dispute to the Society's Secretary for a decision.

12 Protests   Any protest must be made in writing and delivered to the Secretary by the time stated in the schedule.

13 Alteration of exhibits   After judging has taken place no exhibit or part of an exhibit may be altered or removed until the end of the show, except by special permission of the secretary.

14 Liability for loss   All exhibits, personal property, etc, shall be at the risk of the exhibitors and the Society shall not be liable for compensation for loss or damage from any cause whatsoever. Should a show for any cause not be held, no exhibitor shall have any claim on the Society.

Exhibitors will be wholly responsible for all claims made by their own employees under the Common Law or under any statute for compensation arising out of or in the course of such employment for injury or otherwise. The Society has no responsibility to any but its own employees.

15 Right to inspect gardens of exhibitors   In order to be satisfied that the conditions governing competitive exhibits are fulfilled, the Society reserves the right for its official representative to visit by appointment, before or after a show, gardens from which plants, flowers, fruit or vegetables have been entered for competition.

SUGGESTIONS ON ORGANISATION

1 The classification of exhibitors   It is recommended that organisers make it clear whether or not the show is to be open to amateurs only or also to professionals *(see definitions in the Glossary, p155 and p161)*.

The definition of amateur allows an amateur who employs a full-time gardener to compete in the show. If that is not the intention, it is recommended that the schedule states: "The show is open to amateurs who do not employ a gardener for more than 10 hours per week."

2 Exhibits from professional gardeners   Anyone who is employed as a gardener, either full- or part-time, should be allowed to exhibit in his/her own name only produce from his/her own private garden or allotment. Produce from an employer's garden should be exhibited in the employer's name.

3 Division of duties: suggested responsibilities of officials

Show Secretaries
- Book the venue well in advance.
- Arrange the tabling.
- Appoint judges.
- Arrange publicity.
- Arrange for entry-takers.
- Appoint stewards and ensure they are familiar with their duties *(see pp16–17, paragraph 9)*.
- Be familiar with the show's rules and be responsible for their implementation.
- Ensure that the hall is open and ready for staging at the right time and remains open until the stated completion time.
- Mark out the show benches.
- Provide entry-cards.
- Provide vases, plates, etc if available.
- Interpret the wording of the schedule if required and inform the judges of the ruling before they begin judging.
- If any classes (such as onions) have a weight limit, make available an accurate set of scales for the use of exhibitors, stewards and judges, both before and during judging.
- Immediately before judging starts, draw together judges and stewards and explain layout, duties and sections to all concerned.

- Ensure that the judge or judges are available to receive and act upon protests in a timely fashion.
- Be familiar with the show schedule, and direct the provision of advice and the fair hearing of disputes and protests.
- Ensure that prize-monies are paid promptly after the show and that any trophies and special prizes reach their respective winners as quickly as possible.

Stewards
- Assist new exhibitors uncertain of classification or procedure.
- See that exhibitors put the right exhibit in the right class and ensure that it is staged according to schedule.
- Ensure each exhibit has its proper entry-card correctly displayed.
- Check weights/sizes, container dimensions or space and advise judges where entries are not in accordance with the schedule.
- Check immediately prior to judging that every exhibit has been staged according to the schedule and remove any coverings.
- Draw to the judges' attention any exhibit that appears to be not according to schedule.
- Advise judges of any special awards or prizes. Check that every exhibit in each class has been judged.
- Affix prize labels to entry cards after judging.

Judges
- Assess all exhibits as shown and award prizes as stated in the schedule including any special awards.
- Refer to steward and/or show secretary any exhibits that are wrongly staged, incorrectly labelled or not according to schedule. Write a note explaining why an exhibit has been adjudged to be "Not According to Schedule" unless it is deemed preferable to speak to the exhibitor privately after the judging is completed.
- Be available to receive and act upon protests in a timely fashion.
- Correct wrong names and, wherever possible, add the name to a label that bears the words "name unknown".
- Advise the show secretary after the show of ways in which the schedule could be improved.

4 Entry-cards and prize cards   Every exhibit should have an entry-card provided by the show secretary. A card 150 × 120mm is suitable. The face of the card should bear the name of the Society and/or Show and should have places for the number and description of the class, the name of the exhibitor, the name of the gardener (if any) and also a place where a label may be affixed if the exhibit should win a prize or be commended.

The back of the card should have places for the class number and the exhibitor's number and also a place for the judges to write the award given.

All the above-mentioned particulars, except the judges' assessment, should be on the card when it is handed to the exhibitor on arrival to stage exhibits. Each exhibitor should be responsible for the placing of the correct card with each of his/her exhibits, face downwards. A steward should see that this is done.

As soon as practicable after all judging has been completed, including Best in Show, all the cards should be turned face upwards and relevant prize or commendation labels affixed. It is recommended that the conventional colour code for prize cards is followed: red for first prize, blue for second prize and green or yellow for third prize.

5 Labelling exhibits The general appearance of a show is improved if all exhibits are labelled and it is recommended that exhibitors are provided with labels by the secretary. White cards about 75 × 25mm are suitable. Labels are best written or typed in capital letters.

6 Judges The qualifications of a good judge are integrity, familiarity with the kinds and cultivars of the classes to be adjudicated and a knowledge of the skill required to grow and stage them. Good judges for a horticultural show are most frequently to be found among those people who are or have been successful exhibitors. Lists of qualified judges are available from specialist societies and county judges' guilds. To view the RHS Register of Judges, visit:
www.rhs.org.uk/Learning/Publications/registers/index.htm

To avoid unconscious bias, judges for a local show should be drawn from outside the area that the show serves.

The number of judges should be determined by the number of classes and the time available for judging. The ideal number for a group of judges is three. If one group is not enough the ideal is to have two or more groups of three. Whilst it is ideal to have teams of three judges, cost may preclude this for smaller shows. Where there are two judges, it is advisable to appoint a referee to give a casting vote if required.

One judge in each group should be nominated as responsible for the written record of the decisions of the group.

7 Referee or referees   Some shows, particularly those with strong competitions, require final decisions where judgements are in doubt. A referee or referees may be appointed with all the qualifications of experienced judges. In the absence of a referee, societies should nominate an experienced person who is not exhibiting to arbitrate or confirm unresolved judgements.

8 Clearing show for judging   Before judging starts the venue should be cleared of everyone except those authorised by the committee to be present. Normally no exhibitor should be authorised to remain.

9 Stewards   Stewarding is an important function at any show. The steward is the link with the judge, the exhibitors and the show secretary. A steward's duties provide a very good training ground for those who wish to become either exhibitors or judges. One or more stewards should be appointed to ensure, as far as possible, that all exhibits are according to the schedule and that the judges have nothing to do beyond their proper duties. A steward should not be asked to officiate in any section where he/she is an exhibitor.

If the number of entries in a class causes congestion in the space allotted on the show bench to the detriment of the exhibits, the steward should report the problem to the show organizer who will endeavour to adjust the spacing. Any change should be done with extreme care so as not to alter in any way the exhibitor's own staging.

There are several important requirements for which stewards are responsible. These are summarized in this paragraph and in paragraph 3 under *Stewards (see p14).* Stewards should not have an interest in the particular section being judged or comment on the work of judging. At all times stewards should keep at a discreet distance from the judge. Stewards should make no comment except to answer any administrative queries raised by the judge, nor should they take part in any technical aspects of judging. Before the judging begins the stewards should see that everyone leaves the show venue except those authorised by the committee to be present during the judging. When judges indicate that a class has been judged, the steward or a recorder is responsible for seeing that prize stickers are fixed to the class cards; that comments on why a class/exhibit has been marked NAS have been made on the appropriate cards; and where points cards were used, that they have been completed by the judges.

Prize cards should only be up-turned after judges have decided the Best Exhibit/Exhibits in the section/show or any special prizes. Finally, class cards must not be up-turned to

16

display the appropriate prize sticker until all judging, including Best Exhibits, has been completed. When the show is open to the public, the presence of stewards is invaluable to patrol sections and stop theft and the handling of exhibits.

An experienced steward is a great asset to a show.

10 Recording entries and prizewinners It is important that accurate records are made to record the names of exhibitors and the awards obtained. Many societies use a database programme or spreadsheets on a laptop computer.

- On receipt of entries, it is advisable to give exhibitors an entry number.
- This number, with the name of the exhibitor, is entered on the entry card, together with details of the class entered. The class number and exhibitor number only are also written on the back of the entry card.
- The Royal Horticultural Society currently uses a manual system whereby each team of judges is issued with a judges' card, denoting the classes given to them. This card has horizontal lines and seven vertical columns which, from left to right, are headed "Class", "1st Prize", "2nd Prize", "3rd Prize", "4th Prize", "HC" and "C." When the judges have completed each class, they enter the numbers of the prizewinners, and when all the classes have been judged, the judges sign the card and hand it to the Show Organiser, together with a note of any special awards given.
- Some show organisers appoint stewards to record a list of the prizewinners.
- It is important that the show organisers use a system to record the entries made, the points and prize money attained, and any special awards given.
- A series of spreadsheets may be used (one for each section), or the details may be recorded in a book.

11 Multiple-entry classes Societies may retain the option of allowing multiple-entry classes and making all entries eligible for all prizes but this is only advisable when the organisers can be sure of strong support from a large number of exhibitors and a high standard of entries. There is no reason why a show schedule should not contain one or more multiple-entry classes while retaining the rule of one entry per exhibitor in the rest of the schedule.

12 Number of entries in a class Show organisers must ensure that judges and exhibitors are not in any doubt about the number of entries that any one individual may enter in any one class. The rule should be that if a exhibitor is only eligible to win one prize in one class then he/she may stage only one entry.

It is the duty of all judges to award the prizes to the most meritorious exhibits in a class and their task should not be complicated by instructions to ignore certain entries because they have all been exhibited by the same exhibitor. The public, too, will not readily understand why second and third prizes in such classes have gone to exhibits that are clearly inferior to others that have received no prizes at all.

13 The withholding of prizes It is recommended that Rule 9 regarding the withholding of prizes be adopted, but the power to withhold a prize should be exercised sparingly as the whole object in offering prizes is to encourage exhibitors. If none of the exhibits in a class is worthy of the first prize, it is sometimes advisable to award the second prize for the best exhibit and the third prize for that which is next in order of merit. The judges may be empowered to decide whether an exhibit in a class is worthy of the prize but where a trophy is offered for the best exhibit in a section or in the whole show it may be advisable to ask the judges to make a recommendation and for the committee to reserve the decision to itself.

It is not desirable that a prize should be withheld solely on the ground that the exhibits are few in number. If an exhibit is worthy of the prize, the prize should be awarded, for it is not the exhibitor's fault that others have failed to exhibit.

14 Best Bloom A special award for the Best Bloom shown in the horticultural classes may be required. For the purposes of such a competition, the strict definition of a bloom as a single open bloom or a flowerhead should be disregarded, so as to render eligible single spikes or inflorescences of such plants as delphiniums, gladioli and pelargoniums.

15 Best in Show It is difficult for judges to decide between the best fruit or vegetable exhibit, but almost impossible to decide between these and handicraft, floral art and domestic exhibits. If a Best in Show award is required it is strongly recommended that the award is limited to horticultural exhibits only. Even then, it is often a problem to decide, especially where there are several judges involved in different sections of the show. It is better that awards are given for Best Vegetable, Best Flower and Best Fruit exhibits.

- Where a society wishes to provide a Best in Show award, then the judges should each point their own Best in Section on a highest percentage basis prior to the judges assembling together to award Best in Show. Similarly, in awarding a Best in Section award, judges should point possible winners.
- A disqualified exhibit cannot be eligible for consideration for Best in Show but may be eligible for the award of a special prize at the discretion of the show committee.
- Individual dishes in collection classes are not eligible for Best in Show awards as they cannot be considered as exhibits in themselves, only as part of an exhibit.

16 Protests   The time by which protests (which should be required to be in writing) must be received by the secretary should be stated in the schedule and should be such that it is possible to consult the judges about any protests that concern their decisions or necessitate their reviewing any of the classes. The committee should, however, be willing to consider at any time a protest that alleges fraud.

In some circumstances it may be desirable to state in the schedule that any protest must be accompanied by a cash deposit which will be returned if the protest is considered by the committee to be justified.

The organisers should ensure that the judge or judges are available to receive and act upon protests in a timely fashion.

17 Disputes   When the committee of a local horticultural society is unable to resolve a problem connected with a show, the matter in dispute may be submitted to the Royal Horticultural Society. The enquiry should be sent by the secretary and not by any individual member of the local society. The letter, which must enclose a schedule of the show and give all the relevant facts, should be addressed to:

The Secretary, The Royal Horticultural Society, 80 Vincent Square, London SW1P 2PE.

18 Hardy plants   Classes are often provided for "hardy" plants. A hardy plant is one that is able to survive the average winter when grown in the open without protection but plants that can be grown in the open in some parts of the British Isles need shelter under glass in colder districts. If any question arises on this point in a competition, the exhibitor should be required to sign a statement that the plant in question has been grown in the open, without protective covering, for at least the twelve months before the show.

19 Liability for injury to members of the public, guests, exhibitors and voluntary staff Organisers of flower shows are liable for injury suffered by anyone visiting or participating in the show and if the Society does not have public liability insurance cover then the liability lies with the officers of that Society who may be proceeded against. It is therefore essential that cover is provided either by the owners of the hall or building in which the show is held or by taking out a special policy on behalf of the Society.

20. Right to inspect gardens or allotments of exhibitors If, as is recommended, a society has a rule *(see p12, paragraph 15)* reserving the right to inspect the gardens of exhibitors and it is decided to exercise that right, it does not follow that the gardens of any other exhibitors need be visited.

SUGGESTIONS TO SCHEDULE-MAKERS

1 The use of terms   Anyone concerned with the drafting of a schedule should become familiar with the definition of terms in common use and especially with the meaning of "kinds" and "cultivars" (varieties). *(See Glossary, pp159–160 and p156.)*

2 The timetable   The following dates and times should be clearly stated in the schedule:
- The latest time for the receipt of entries.
- The time when staging can be started and the time by which it must be completed.
- The time judging will commence.
- The time when the show will be open for the admission of exhibitors and the public after the judging has been finished.
- The time by which protests should be made.
- The time when the show closes and when exhibitors may start to remove their exhibits.
- The time by which all exhibits and property of exhibitors must be removed.
- The date by which prize money will be paid.

3 The enforcement of rules   It is not advisable to print such warnings as "This rule will be strictly enforced", as such expressions imply that other rules will not be enforced.

4 The time for the receipt of entries   In order to obtain the maximum number of entries it is advisable to make the last day for the receipt of entries as late as possible, but sufficient time must be allowed between the receipt of entries and the staging of exhibits to allow the necessary clerical work to be done and the spaces for the various classes to be worked out. The interval between the last day for the receipt of entries and the opening day of the show should not, as a rule, be more than a week. It is sometimes advisable for the regulation on the matter to say: "All entries should reach the secretary not later than (date) but the Secretary may, at his/her discretion, accept a late entry up to, but not after, the day before the show."

5 Rules   It is strongly recommended that the rules under which the show is to be conducted should be clearly stated in full in the schedule. These would normally be the rules set out

on *pp10–12* of this *Handbook*, with such additional rules as
may be necessary.

Where certain classes are to be judged according to
Specialist Society rules, it is important to mention this in
the schedule.

6 Constitution of exhibits   It is important that the schedule
should make clear how many specimens constitute an exhibit.
For fruit and vegetables the quantities ordinarily required at
the Royal Horticultural Society's shows are detailed on *p49* and
pp70–72. These quantities are also suitable for the leading
regional shows. Individual schedule makers may wish to
reduce these quantities to suit the size and scope of their own
shows. These quantities can be printed in tables similar to
those on *p49* and *pp70–72*, or in the wording of each class.

In the case of collections it is recommended that a general
rule is included as follows:

"Every dish must consist of one cultivar (variety) only,
unless otherwise stated in the schedule. The numbers of
specimens constituting dishes in a collection of fruit or
vegetables must be those specified in the single-dish classes,
unless otherwise specified in the schedule."

7 The relative value of prizes   As far as possible the relative
value of first, second and third prizes should be consistent
throughout the schedule.

Thus if a 5:3:2 ratio is adopted and the first prize is, for
example, £5, then the second should be £3, the third £2 and
the fourth (if a fourth prize is awarded) £1.

The value of the prizes in a class should be related to what
is involved in producing the required exhibit.

8 The point-value of prizes   When a cup or other trophy is
offered for award to the most successful competitor in a show
or in a section of a show, a competitor's degree of success is
usually assessed by giving a point-value to the prizes.

The number of points should be graduated in much
the same way as money prizes are graduated and the point-
value of the prizes in the various classes should be stated
in the schedule.

9 The withholding of prizes   It is desirable that an
appropriate standard for prizes should be established and
should not be allowed to deteriorate. In order to do this it is
recommended that Rule 9 *(p11)* should be adopted, so that if
the best exhibit in a class is not worthy of the first prize, the
first prize need not be awarded. Similarly, the rule empowers

the judges to withhold the second or, indeed, any prize. Whether a prize is awarded or not should depend solely on the merits of the exhibit.

10 More than one entry from a competitor in a class

The practice of allowing competitors to stage more than one entry in a class, yet only be eligible for one prize, causes practical difficulties, both to the judges and organisers, and also confusion to the public visiting the show. Schedule-makers are strongly recommended not to adopt such a practice. *(See pp17–18, paragraphs 11 and 12.)*

11 The numbering of classes

To avoid the possibility of confusion, the classes should be numbered in consecutive order (except as mentioned below) throughout a schedule; that is to say, no class number should appear twice.

When a schedule contains two or more sections, it may be helpful in avoiding unnecessary alterations and consequent expense in subsequent years if some numbers are omitted. Thus if Section I ends at Class 15, Section II might begin at Class 21 and so on. This would allow anything up to five classes to be added to Section I without necessitating the renumbering of the classes in Section II.

12 Salading and salad vegetables

These are vegetables used as articles of food in either a raw or cooked state and served cold in salads. The kinds that may be used for horticultural-show purposes are listed under "Salading or salad vegetable" in the *Glossary, p162.*

If it is desired that each exhibit in a class should consist of four kinds of such vegetables , then the schedule should call for "Four kinds of salading or salad vegetables, 1 dish of each".

13 The use of the terms "genus", "species" and "hybrid"

For the purposes of competitions at the majority of horticultural shows the words "kind" and "cultivar" are recommended as being not only adequate but also the most easily understood terms to use in the classification of flowers and ornamental plants as well as fruit and vegetables. However, those terms are not always sufficiently precise for competitions in connection with alpines, cacti, orchids, succulents, shrubs or trees. For such competitions the terms "genus", "species" and "hybrid" may also be used.

14 "Distinct", "similar" and "dissimilar"

It is recommended that the words "distinct", "similar" and "dissimilar" are not used in the specifications for classes in schedules. Their use is undesirable because they lack precision, for what is "distinct" to one person is not to another.

15 "Should" and "must"   The word "should" is often used where "must" is intended and vice versa. "Should" leaves what follows optional; "must" makes what follows obligatory. The inadvertent substitution of the one word for the other may cause an exhibit to be disqualified or free it from liability to disqualification.

16 The ripeness of fruit   Unless the schedule states otherwise apples, pears and gooseberries may be shown either ripe or unripe. Nevertheless, where classes for apples, pears or gooseberries are included in a show and the schedule does not specify that the fruit must be ripe, preference should be given, all things being equal, to cultivars in season rather than to larger or more showy cultivars that have been picked prematurely.

17 Dual-purpose apples   Some cultivars of apples are classified as dual-purpose *(see pp64–68)*. It is recommended that the schedule state that when dual-purpose apples are shown as cooking apples they should be more than 80mm in diameter and when shown as dessert apples, they should not exceed 80mm in diameter.

18 Annuals and biennials   Many perennial plants are commonly cultivated as annuals; that is to say, they are raised from seed, flowered and discarded within twelve months. The difficulty of distinguishing between annuals, biennials and perennials is so great that it is recommended that instead of having a class or classes calling for annuals and/or biennials, such classes should call for "flowers raised from seed during the twelve months preceding the Show". In such a class it would be permissible to exhibit not only true annuals and biennials but also perennials (such as antirrhinums and petunias) which are often cultivated as annuals.

19 Perennials   Where a class invites the exhibition of a vase of more than one stem of a perennial plant, it is recommended that the wording of the schedule makes it clear that these should be of similar kinds, for example woody, herbaceous or bulbous.

20 Beans   It is often impossible to distinguish climbing from dwarf French beans and they are considered as one kind for exhibition purposes.

21 Beetroot, carrot and potato classes   Exhibitors and judges are often in doubt about the cultivars that may be shown without fear of disqualification in classes for these vegetables. This uncertainty may in part be caused by different views about the classification of cultivars (either by shape or by colour) and also by the use of wording in classes that is open to an unduly limiting interpretation. Opinions may differ as to the identity of "intermediate" carrots or "kidney-shaped" potatoes; exhibitors may not know in which classes in a show they should be entered and judges may disqualify them for being in the wrong classes.

Schedule-makers are accordingly advised to adopt as simple wording as possible for beetroot, carrot and potato classes. The Royal Horticultural Society provides two classes for each vegetable in addition to collection classes. "Intermediate" carrots are classed as long, pointed types. No attempt is made to provide separate potato classes for each of the different shapes nor is a rigid colour classification given. If an exhibitor has specimens of a normally "coloured" cultivar of potato that show no colour, he/she is able to show them in the "white class". Suitable wording where more than one class for beetroot, carrots and potatoes is required is:

Beetroot, globe
Beetroot, long
Beetroot, cylindrical or globe other than dark red
  eg 'Chioggia' or 'Golden'
Carrots, long
Carrots, stump rooted
Potatoes, white, of any shape
Potatoes, other than white, of any shape

22 Onion classes   Schedule-makers are recommended not to use such wording as "Onions, spring-sown cultivars", "Onions, autumn-sown cultivars", or "Onions, cultivars grown from sets" as these can lead to uncertainty. Difficulties occur when separate classes of this kind are included, as judges are often unable to determine the origin or method of culture of bulbs entered for classes under these headings. When wording onion classes it is advisable to consider examples similar to the following:

Onions, 1 dish
Onions, excluding green salad or pickling onions, 1 dish
Onions, no bulb to exceed 250g, 1 dish

23 Tomato classes   Because it is often difficult for judges to distinguish between indoor- and outdoor-grown tomatoes where the latter have had some form of protection, such as plastic sheeting, it is suggested that schedule-makers make no distinction between indoor- and outdoor-grown tomatoes.

24 The size of pot   The diameter of a pot or pan is the inside measurement made as close to the top as possible. With square or rectangular pots the area is expressed in square centimetres (or square inches) calculated by measuring straight across the top at right angles to the rim. Where the manufacturer's stamp is embossed on the pot this should be accepted. (Where schedule-makers are prepared to admit both circular and rectangular pots in the same class they should state the maximum dimension of both that would be acceptable or give the volume.)

25 Foliage   Unless otherwise stated, in flower classes the use of foliage is optional but if used must be from the kind (genus), but need not be of the cultivar, being shown. This should be clarified in the schedule.

26 The use of the words "and" and "or"   Schedules sometimes contain classes such as "Hardy and Half-hardy flowers, 3 kinds, 1 vase of each". If in such a class an exhibitor staged three kinds of hardy flowers it would not be according to the schedule; nor would an exhibit consisting of three kinds of half-hardy flowers.

If the intention is to allow
a an exhibit consisting solely of hardy flowers; and
b an exhibit consisting solely of half-hardy flowers; and
c an exhibit consisting partly of hardy and partly of half-hardy flowers, then the class should read:
"HARDY AND/OR HALF-HARDY FLOWERS, 3 kinds, 1 vase of each."

27 The wording of classes   It is very important that the wording of classes leaves no doubt in the minds of exhibitors and judges as to the schedule-maker's intention for each class. Examples of how to avoid confusion are as follows:

Cultivars/kinds
• If the intention is to have a class of three different cultivars of dessert apple, the class should read "APPLES, 3 DESSERT CULTIVARS, 1 dish of each".
• A class reading "VEGETABLES, A COLLECTION OF 4 DISHES" would allow up to four dishes of, for example, potatoes.
  If different kinds are required, the class would read
  "VEGETABLES, A COLLECTION OF 4 KINDS, 1 dish of each".

- Alternatively, if the schedule-maker will allow (say) two dishes of the same kind of vegetable in the class, the class should read "VEGETABLES, A COLLECTION OF 4 DISHES, not more than 2 dishes of any 1 kind". This would allow two dishes of the same cultivar of (say) potato and two dishes of the same cultivar of (say) cabbage.
  If this is not intended, the class should read "VEGETABLES, A COLLECTION OF 4 CULTIVARS, not more than 2 dishes of any 1 kind".
- A class reading "POTATOES, 3 DISHES" would allow two or three dishes of the same cultivar to be shown.
  If different cultivars are required, the class should read "POTATOES, 3 CULTIVARS, 1 dish of each".

In each of the above examples, it is assumed that the schedule will contain a table showing the quantities required. If not, it would be necessary to state the quantities required (*ie* "1 dish of 4 of each").

Dahlias

- The wording for a vase of five dahlias where the exhibitor can show any number of cultivars of dahlia in one vase should read "DAHLIAS, 1 or more cultivars, 1 vase of 5".
- If you wish to be a little more specialist and limit the class to blooms of cactus or semi-cactus dahlias, the class should read "DAHLIAS, CACTUS AND/OR SEMI-CACTUS, 1 or more cultivars, 1 vase of 5".
- If you wish to be even more specialist and to allow only small flowers and only 1 cultivar, the class should read "DAHLIAS, SMALL CACTUS OR SEMI-CACTUS, 1 cultivar, 1 vase of 5".

Annuals

- For flowers that are generally grown as annuals, the class should read "FLOWERS GROWN FROM SEED IN THE PRECEDING 12 MONTHS, 1 vase". This wording would allow any number of mixed kinds and does not state the quantity required. The class may also state that, say, three kinds are required and also limit the number of stems to (say) ten. It would then read "FLOWERS GROWN FROM SEED IN THE PRECEDING 12 MONTHS, 3 kinds, 1 vase of 10 stems".

Perennials

- If a class reads "PERENNIAL FLOWERS, 1 vase" it would allow herbaceous perennials, trees and shrubs to be shown as well as hardy and half-hardy perennials. It would also allow any number of kinds and cultivars.
- More suitable classes would be:

"HARDY HERBACEOUS PERENNIALS IN BLOOM, 1 vase";
"TREES AND/OR SHRUBS IN BLOOM, 1 vase";
"HARDY HERBACEOUS PERENNIALS IN BLOOM, 3 vases, 1 kind of each".

General perennial classes

- If there are individual classes for (say) roses, and the schedule-maker wishes to exclude them from the more general perennial classes, the class should read: "TREES AND/OR SHRUBS IN BLOOM, excluding roses, 1 vase".

28 Any other fruit/vegetable classes These classes are intended to allow exhibitors to show fruit or vegetables that they are not able to enter in any other class in the schedule. The items shown are normally those for which the schedule-makers feel there would be insufficient entries to justify the particular fruit or vegetable having a class of its own.

Within such a class there is the probability that a wide diversity of kinds will be entered each with a different point value according to the recommendations given on *pp50–103*. Points are based to a large extent on the degree of difficulty involved in producing a high quality crop for the show bench and it is not desirable that fruits or vegetables that command high points should be judged against those that are easy to grow and therefore command low points. To avoid this situation schedule-makers are advised to include two "any other" classes as follows:

Any other fruit/vegetable with a point value of up to 14.
Any other fruit/vegetable with a point value of 15 or more.

It is appreciated that in small shows on a restricted budget there might only be sufficient prize-money for one "any other" class and where this is the case the judge concerned should be asked to make due allowance for the degree of difficulty of cultivation in his/her assessment. The pointing system should only be used as a guide in such classes and other factors such as quality and presentation should be taken into consideration.

SUGGESTIONS TO EXHIBITORS

1 The schedule An exhibitor should read the schedule very carefully, including all the rules. If anything is not clear he/she should contact the show secretary immediately. The solution of problems should not be left until the show day, as exhibitors and officials are then particularly busy.

2 Dates and times The dates and times given in the schedule should be carefully noted, particularly:

a   the latest day and time for the receipt of entries;

b   the time when staging may be started and the hour by which it must be finished; and

c   the time when the show closes and the hour by which exhibitors must have removed their property.

In his/her own interest every exhibitor should do his/her utmost to adhere to the timetable and avoid doing things at the last moment.

3 Entry-form An exhibitor should see that his/her intentions are stated quite clearly on the entry-form, that the name and address are legible and that the form reaches the secretary by the appointed day but earlier if possible. If the entries arrive over a period of a week or so it is much easier to cope with the secretarial work than if nearly all the entries arrive on the last day.

4 Prizes are not everything When selecting the classes in which to compete, an exhibitor should bear in mind that there is more honour in exhibiting in a strongly contested class without winning a prize than in winning a prize in a class where there is little or no competition.

5 Avoid making too many entries No exhibitor should put in an entry for a class unless he/she is reasonably sure that he/she will be able to stage an exhibit in it. Those who make numerous entries and fail to produce the exhibits or cancel the entries at the last moment make it difficult or impossible for the staging to be allocated as it should be, with the result that in some classes the exhibits are crowded and elsewhere there are vacant spaces.

6 Encourage beginners If, when looking through a schedule, it occurs to an exhibitor that a friend is a successful grower of some particular flower, fruit or vegetable for which there is a class, the friend should be persuaded to enter. If the friend has never exhibited before and needs advice, he/she should be helped as much as possible. Similarly, if when staging exhibits a beginner is encountered, the experienced exhibitor should give any assistance needed. If, when putting up exhibits, one exhibitor notices that another has inadvertently made a mistake (such as staging the wrong number of specimens or omitting to put labels or entry-cards in position) attention should be drawn to the matter while there is time for it to be put right.

7 Allow ample time for staging   Plenty of time should be allowed for putting up exhibits and for finishing off well before the time scheduled for the completion of staging. A last-minute rush should be avoided as this is when mistakes are likely to occur.

8 Labels and entry-cards   Labels with the names of the cultivars to be exhibited should be prepared at home in order to save time on the show day. It is best to use block capitals. On arrival at the place of the exhibition an exhibitor should immediately procure entry-cards from the secretary or whoever has been deputed to deal with them. Both labels and entry-cards should be placed on the exhibits in good time and care should be taken to see that they correspond to the exhibits.

9 "Should" and "must"   As many schedule-makers inadvertently put "should" when they mean "must" and many judges do not distinguish between the meanings of the two words, if the schedule says "should" it is often wise for an exhibitor to act, if possible, as if the word were "must".

10 The number of specimens required   Particular attention should be paid to the number of specimens for which the schedule asks, as an exhibit consisting of either more or less will be liable to disqualification ("Not According to Schedule").

11 Uniformity of specimens constituting an exhibit   In any competitive exhibit uniformity of all the characteristics of the specimens constituting the exhibit is important. Therefore it is unwise to weaken an exhibit by mixing, for example, large specimens with others that are smaller.

12 Selection of cultivars   Some cultivars are naturally better for horticultural-show purposes than others. Exhibitors are advised to visit other shows and to make a note of those cultivars that are successful. Other useful sources of information are experienced exhibitors and national specialist societies.

13 Be absent during judging   If they have not already done so, at the time fixed for the completion of staging, all exhibitors should leave the show venue and not return until the time fixed for re-admission.

14 The judges' decision   The judges' decision, whatever it may be, should be accepted with good grace.

15 Protests   These should not be made lightly but only if, after careful consideration, an exhibitor feels sure that a mistake has been made. In those circumstances an appeal should be made in writing to the secretary. The final decision should be accepted without question.

If, however, the time fixed in the schedule for the receipt of protests has passed, the judges' decision should be accepted without comment and no action taken.

16 Liability for loss   The organisers usually stipulate in the schedule that exhibits and other property of exhibitors will at all times be at the risk of the exhibitors. It is impossible for the organisers to ensure the safety of exhibitors' property especially when exhibits are being removed at the close of a show. Therefore each exhibitor should arrange to take charge of his/her exhibits immediately after the show closes and if he/she cannot do so personally, arrangements should be made beforehand for someone else to do so.

17 The preparation and presentation of produce at shows   All exhibits should be staged as attractively as possible in accordance with the rules and schedule. In close competition points for arrangement may be the deciding factor, and a judge cannot fail to be favourably influenced by good presentation. Always take a few extra specimens to the show in case of accident, and before leaving the show bench check that the correct numbers have been staged so that your exhibit is not marked NAS ("not according to schedule").

18 The preparation and presentation of flowers *(See also paragraph 17 above)*
• **Preparation before cutting**   Starting two or three weeks before a show, keep the soil moist by giving generous quantities of water at each application, especially if the

weather is hot and dry. In many cases the removal of unwanted weak sideshoots or buds will aid development of the central or main flowers. If possible, and permissible under the schedule, protect blooms such as asters, chrysanthemums, dahlias, gladioli, lilies and pansies to prevent spotting caused by heavy rain, hail damage or splashing from the soil. If light conditions are not good, make sure pot plants have sufficient space in which to develop and turn the pots frequently to avoid lop-sided growth. Pot plants such as calceolarias and cinerarias should be lightly shaded otherwise there is a risk of the flowers fading in colour or scorching.

• **Cutting** Before cutting and exhibiting, carefully study the show schedule and note the requirements for each class you intend to enter. Cut for a show in the evening or early morning when the flowers and foliage are cool and not affected by heat. Flower stems should be cut as long as possible. Make a slanting cut at the end of the stalk as this will assist the uptake of water. Certain flowers, *eg* some cultivars of chrysanthemums and penstemons, are particularly reluctant to absorb water and in these cases slitting the cut stems 75mm upwards from the base or dipping the severed ends in boiling water will improve matters. Other plants, notably poppies, do not seal easily after cutting and should have their stalk ends seared in a naked flame to prevent wilting.

As cutting proceeds, carefully label each item, for mistakes easily occur that can affect your chances in competition and cause disappointment. Avoid handling show material any more than is necessary. Carry the cut stems with blooms facing downwards, keeping the plants away from draughts or bright sunshine as much as possible. Try to cut sufficient material to allow some latitude when final selection is made at the time the exhibit is staged.

When cutting is completed, remove undeveloped side-shoots, unopened buds and some of the lower leaves as these will often divert water from the stems and open flowers to be exhibited. The cut stems should be plunged upright up to their necks in deep containers of clean water. It is a considerable advantage to do this overnight, placing the containers in a cool position from which light is mostly excluded because stems are drawn towards the light and consequently they can become curved or bent. If this is not possible, wrap a sheet of newspaper round the material and tie at the top to exclude light. Take care to see the covering paper is tied well above the uppermost flowers and that it does not absorb any water from the container. Flowers treated in this way will be encouraged to expand before a show begins. Pot plants should receive enough water so they are fresh at the time of showing.

Where the show schedule permits, stems of plants in this section are neatly tied, using individual supports that should be made as inconspicuous as possible.

• **Transit to a show**   Place the material, either flat or upright, in containers of sufficient size to prevent the flowers becoming squashed or damaged during the journey. Pack cotton wool, soft paper or other similar material between specimens to prevent movement and buffeting in transport. Ensure that pot plants are securely supported to prevent excessive sway and subsequent breakage. Always allow enough time for the journey so that if delay should occur there will still be time to stage the exhibit without undue haste.

• **Staging exhibits at a show**   Remove any damaged flowers together with discoloured or broken leaves that may have occurred as a result of the journey. Cut a portion from the base of all flower stems to assist the uptake of water, making sure that the length of stalk retained is appropriate for the size of vase or container you propose to use. Check that all containers are filled with water otherwise plants in your exhibit may wilt during the show. Strive to produce exhibits of good balance with flowers of even size and quality that are accommodated in containers of suitable proportions. Label exhibits clearly, preferably using block capital letters for cultivar (variety) names but defer this operation until last if it is intended to apply a final spray of water over the exhibit just before judging starts.

Delphiniums Delphinium spikes are preferably shown with sideshoots removed.

Roses, cluster-flowered Select floriferous stems and remove the central bud of each cluster as early as possible (leaving this until the central bloom has unfurled may leave a gap in the centre of the cluster). Cut the stems before the show at a time appropriate to the cultivar. Experience will enable you to produce perfect clusters by experimenting with disbudding and time of cutting. All underdeveloped laterals should be neatly removed. The cut should be at an oblique angle to the stem. Place in as deep a receptacle as possible and leave in a cool dark place.

Roses, large-flowered Select strong stems and a bud that is likely to produce a flower that is at its best on the day of the show (experience can enable this to be carried out to perfection, remembering that different cultivars and different weather conditions may affect the timing). Remove the side buds. Blooms can be 'dressed' when still in growth. This can be done by carefully unfurling the petals and serious exhibitors often place 'pellets' between the rows of petals to ensure a circular outline, but must remember to remove the pellets before staging the blooms. The placing of pellets is unnecessary for small shows. Do not over-dress blooms so that they lose their natural shape. The judges will be looking for average-sized blooms in most classes but above-average size in classes for specimen blooms and in 'box' classes. See **Roses, cluster-flowered** (above) for advice on cutting and storing before the show.

19 The preparation and presentation of fruit
(See also p31, paragraph 17)
• **Preparation**   Initial preparation should begin well beforehand. Protect against frost and cold winds in spring: both may destroy, mar or blemish all kinds of fruit. Thinning is often necessary where a heavy set of fruit occurs. Apples, pears, plums, peaches, apricots, figs, grapes, gooseberries and strawberries all benefit from thinning. Thin in stages, especially those kinds of fruit that shed some of their fruitlets naturally, *eg* apples and pears, bearing in mind that early thinning has the most beneficial effect on size. Remove the small, blemished and misshapen fruits first. With many apple cultivars the "king fruit" or centrally placed apple in the cluster is misshapen.

The fruits that require plenty of sunshine to bring out their characteristic colours should not be over-shaded. As they begin to ripen, they should be exposed gradually to more sunshine by the judicious removal of leaves and the tying back of overhanging foliage. Peaches and nectarines may be tilted towards the sun by means of small pieces of wood placed behind them. There is the risk of sun scald on glasshouse-grown fruits; grapes and figs in particular must have the protection of their foliage. The aim should be to obtain sufficient uniformly ripened specimens for the class or classes to be entered.

Protect against birds well before the fruits ripen. Some growers protect individual fruits in muslin or perforated, clear polythene bags and often the skin finish can be improved in this way. Some fruits are liable to split when almost ripe and others may be spoilt by heavy rains. Black polythene over the soil surface of the rooting area may sometimes mitigate splitting.
• **Picking**   Pick as near to show time as practicable. Before handling it is suggested that the exhibitor's fingernails are trimmed to prevent damage to the produce. Currants, jostaberries and worcesterberries should be picked with the strigs intact choosing the longest strigs with the largest fruits. Grapes should be picked as a complete bunch and each bunch should be cut with a piece of lateral shoot on either side of the stalk to form a T-handle. Melons should be cut in the same

way. Apples, pears, plums and allied fruits, cherries, quinces, figs, medlars, blackberries and allied fruits, gooseberries, raspberries and allied fruits, loganberries and strawberries should be picked with the stalks intact. All nuts when picked should have husks and stalks removed. Apricots, nectarines and peaches should be picked without any attached stalk and stem. Care should be taken not to split the skin in the stalk cavity.

Handle all fruits as little and as gently as possible and by their stalks, where applicable, so that the natural bloom where present, *eg* on grapes, plums and some apples, is not spoilt. Use scissors rather than fingers to remove soft fruits. In wet weather raspberries may be left on the canes and lengths of the fruit-bearing canes brought under cover and placed in water, until dry enough to pick. Strawberries may be kept dry by covering with cloches or by placing individual fruits on the plants in jars but care should be taken to avoid damage by excessive heat.

• **Selection** The desirable qualities of each kind of fruit are set out in the chapter *The Judging of Fruits, pp47–63*. Choose only fruits as near to perfection as can be found. The fruits should be fresh, uniform, free from blemish and characteristic in shape and colour. Refer to the show schedule to see what is required, but pick more than is necessary so that reserves are available when staging. Do not use overripe fruits. Under-ripe fruits should also be avoided, where possible, except where allowed in certain classes *(see p47, Condition)*. Figs with signs of splitting and gages with signs of slight shrivelling can be exhibited as this is a sign of ripeness.

• **Packing** Pack carefully. Wood wool, cotton wool, tissue paper and newspaper are all suitable materials to use. Soft fruits may be damaged by their own weight; avoid packing too many in one container. Hard fruits are best wrapped individually in soft tissue. Keep in a cool place.

• **Presentation and staging** Aim for a neat attractive presentation, symmetrical if possible. Do not polish the fruits. Where applicable, the stalks should always point to the back of the table. In staging small fruits, the well of the plate is best filled with soft tissue paper and then the whole of the top covered, tucking the surplus paper under the plate. Use only white tissue paper, unless otherwise stated in the schedule.

Apples and similar-shaped fruits (including some pears) should be staged with the eye uppermost, stalk end downwards, placing one fruit in the centre and the remainder around it. The centre fruit can be raised by placing a cushion of white tissue beneath it. Do not cut the stalks.

Berries look most attractive if placed in lines so that they can easily be counted. The stalks and calyces should look green and fresh and all point one way. Reject malformed and damaged fruits.

Currants, jostaberries, worcesterberries and blueberries The strigs should be intact and laid roughly parallel, the bottom of the strigs to the front of the plate. Mound the fruit in the centre.

Grapes Unless some other method of staging is specified or permitted by the schedule, glasshouse grapes should be staged on stands and should be pulled well up onto the board. Outdoor grapes grown for winemaking or dessert may be shown on plates.

Most pears, pear-shaped quinces and figs are best arranged around the perimeter of the plate with the stalks towards the centre.

Plums, cherries and similar-shaped fruits are best laid out in lines across the plate. It is important that the bloom is not disturbed and the stalks are intact.

• **Finally**, before leaving the table, clear up any surplus packing material and debris, and check that the entry strictly conforms to the show schedule, is looking its best and is labelled.

20 The preparation and presentation of vegetables
(See also p31, paragraph 17)
All vegetables should be properly prepared for showing. Before handling it is suggested that the exhibitor's fingernails are trimmed to prevent damage to the produce. Where necessary, vegetables should be carefully washed to remove soil but in no circumstances should oils or similar substances be applied in an attempt to enhance their appearance. Wash with a soft cloth and plenty of water; brushing will damage the skin and spoil the appearance of the exhibit. On other kinds retain the natural "bloom" wherever possible. Most vegetables should be given a thorough watering well before harvesting for the show and should be handled carefully during preparations.

Vegetables should be staged as attractively as possible on plates or direct on the table in a "wheel" formation, *eg* peas; in rows, *eg* runner beans; or in pyramidal form, *eg* carrots.

Root vegetables (see p161) must have the leaves cut so that approximately 75mm of leaf stalk remains, which should be neatly tied. With small salad radishes approximately 40mm of stalk should be left. Exhibitors should be aware that in close competition, certain root vegetables may be cut by the judge.

Asparagus peas, mangetout and snap peas Select fresh pods of good colour, that snap easily, and of a size appropriate for the cultivar.

Artichokes, globe Disbud the lateral heads leaving only the large main head. Stage heads on a plate, stalks to the centre.

Aubergines Cut the fruit carefully and stage on a plate, taking care to retain the natural skin condition.

Beans, broad, French and runner Exhibit fresh pods of uniform colour. Stage a uniform-sized exhibit with pods arranged on a plate or directly on the bench; stalks at one end, tails at the other. With all beans it is advisable to check one or two spare pods to assess the condition and interior freshness. Cut all pods from the vine with scissors, ensuring that each pod has a portion of stalk.

It is often impossible to distinguish climbing from dwarf French beans and they are considered as one kind for exhibition purposes.

Beetroot Select roots of even size; for globe beetroot, between 60 and 75mm, for long beetroot as for parsnips; and for cylindrical cultivars, roots approximately 150mm in length. Avoid specimens with poor skin colour at the base of the root or that do not have a single small tap root. Small side roots should be removed. Take care in washing as all marks will show up clearly after a few hours. Trim foliage to approximately 75mm.

Brussels sprouts Cut from the main stem with a knife, all stalks to be nearly the same length. Choose tightly closed sprouts of uniform size. Do not remove too many outer leaves, otherwise depth of colour is reduced.

Cabbages Choose solid heads of equal size, clean and with good waxy bloom. Care should be taken not to mark the bloom. Reject split specimens and any damaged by pests. Remove only a minimum of outer discoloured leaves. Stage with approximately 50mm of stalk remaining, except in collections, and heads towards the front.

Carrots Choose firm, fresh, blemish-free specimens of good even colour and uniformity, without discoloration at the top. Carrots should have the soil or growing medium soaked at the time of lifting to minimise damage to the root. Cut off the foliage to approximately 75mm.

Cauliflowers, calabrese and broccoli, coloured-headed Reject pest-damaged, discoloured, split, loose or uneven-sized heads. Stage with approximately 50mm of stalk remaining, except in collections. Just prior to staging, trim back leaves so that they match the level of the outside of the curd. Cover white curds with clean paper or cloth to exclude light, but remove immediately before the start of judging.

Celery Choose only heads that have no diseased or pest-damaged foliage and that have not been damaged by slugs. Reject specimens with heart rot or with flowerheads forming. Place a tie round the base of the leaves to prevent breaking and clean by a continuous flushing with water; ensure all pests are removed. Before staging, neatly trim off the roots, leaving a pointed butt end. In dish classes where few heads are required, lay them flat on the show bench. In collection classes the specimens are enhanced by display on a backboard. To exclude the light cover with clean paper or damp cloth which must be removed immediately prior to judging.

Courgettes Select young, tender, shapely and uniform fruits approximately 150mm in length and approximately 35mm in diameter, in any colour, or in the case of round cultivars approximately 75mm in diameter. Stage flat with or without flowers still adhering.

Cucumbers Fruits should be completely matched and of a good, fresh green colour. The flower end should be completely developed, the barrel well shaped and with a short handle. Display specimens flat on the show bench. It is not necessary that flowers remain attached.

Fennel, Florence Roots should be neatly trimmed off and foliage trimmed back to approximately 75–100mm, but with terminal foliage retained.

Garlic Clean off all soil fragments, dry completely. Reduce the dried stem to approximately 25mm and remove the roots. Stage bulbs as complete specimens; do not divide into segments (cloves).

Kohlrabi Choose tender, fresh specimens of a size according to cultivar. Trim roots neatly. Cut side foliage back to not more than 50mm and retain the terminal foliage. Stage in clean condition, but do not wash, and retain the natural bloom.

Leeks Specimens should be uniform in length, in good condition and solid (*ie* firm and compact throughout the length of the barrel) and a good, uniform blanch that is not bulbous at the base. Excessive stripping of outer leaves should be avoided, otherwise unsightly ribbing is exposed. In dish classes, preferably stage the leeks to lie flat on the bench with the roots to the front, neatly teased out and well cleaned. Ensure that stem (barrel), leaves (flags) and roots (beard) are flushed clean with tap water which should not be allowed to run between the leaves leaving unsightly soil particles. Avoid soft, discoloured specimens; or evidence in the stem and leaves of rust disease. Place specimens in collections vertically on a backboard, complementing celery, where shown, in length. Bind in the leaves to an appropriate length. Check all specimens for evidence of formation of a flowerhead, rejecting such specimens. Some schedules have classes for intermediate leeks, *ie* where the blanch to the tight button is more than 150mm and less than 350mm. Pot leeks call for a 150mm maximum blanch from root base to "tight button", *ie* the point where the lowest leaf breaks the circumference of the blanched stem. Size should be of a maximum cubic capacity.

• **Nomenclature** used by the National Pot Leek Society:

barrel – the shaft or stem of the plant.

blanch – that part of the stem which is blanched.

button – the point on the barrel of the plant where the lowest leaf breaks the circumference.

flags – the leaves.

veil – a thin white transparent skin that is present across and above the button where the leaf opens out from the sheath and which is included in the measurements.

Lettuce Lift with roots intact in the evening or early morning when the leaves are turgid. Fresh heads of uniform and attractive colour are essential. Roots should be washed, wrapped in moist tissue, inserted in a plastic bag and neatly tied. Wash, avoiding soil particles collecting between the leaves. Remove only markedly damaged outside leaves, and stage laid on the show bench with the hearts facing the front.

Marrows Tender, young, uniform fruits are most desirable, which should be less than 350mm long or, in the case of round cultivars, approximately 500mm in circumference. Old, mature fruits that are not suitable for table use should be excluded. Wipe clean and stage directly on to the show bench.

Onions Avoid soft, stained specimens with thick, immature necks. Do not over skin. Uniform, well-ripened bulbs of good colour are required. Unless otherwise specified by the schedule, the tops should be tied or whipped using uncoloured raffia and the roots neatly trimmed back to the basal plate. Onions are often staged on rings or soft collars. Pickling onions must not exceed 30mm in diameter nor should the necks be tied or whipped.

• **Note**: Onions for early shows, held before 1 July, should have foliage trimmed, excluding onions, green salad.

Onions, green salad The plants should be staged with foliage and roots attached and well washed.

Oriental brassicas, heading types Choose representative

specimens of equal size, clean and with good bloom.
Reject damaged heads and display with roots intact, well
washed, wrapped in moist tissues, inserted in a plastic bag
and neatly tied.

Parsley Should be shown only by itself as a herb. It may
be used as a garnish for a collection of vegetables, but
should receive no points in this case except under the
heading of "arrangement".

Parsnips Roots should be straight and of good length,
evenly tapered and well developed. Great care should be
taken in lifting the roots, as bruising by fingers and scratching
by soil particles will show later. Parsnips should have the soil
or growing medium soaked at the time of lifting to minimise
damage to the root. Wash thoroughly with clean water. Cut
off the foliage to approximately 75mm.

Peas Pods should be uniform in length and in good condition.
Judges will open and check pods during their examination.
When cutting from the vine retain the waxy bloom intact
without finger marks. Gather by cutting with scissors and with
approximately 25mm of stalk, holding the pod at all times by
this. Holding pods up to a strong light will detect internal
damage and reveal the number of peas in the pod.

Peppers, sweet and hot (chilli) Select fruit of the right shape,
size and colour for the cultivar. Fruit may be shown immature
but fully formed, usually green, or at the mature or coloured
stage. The exhibit should be uniform in colour.

Potatoes Select medium-sized specimens, generally between
175g and 225g. Select equally matched tubers with shallow
eyes. Freedom from skin blemishes that may be caused by
pests, diseases or careless handling is essential. The tubers
should be very carefully washed in ample, clean water with a
soft sponge – on no account use a coarse cloth or brush. Stage
on plates with the rose end outwards; cover with a cloth to
exclude light until judging commences.

Pumpkins A well-formed specimen, mature and of good colour.

Radishes, small salad The body of the radish should be fresh,
firm, medium-sized, young, tender and brightly coloured. It
should be free from blemishes and with foliage trimmed to
approximately 40mm. Dig at the last possible moment to
retain maximum turgidity. Cut spare specimens to check
internal condition.

Rhubarb Stalks should be fresh, straight, long and tender with
well-developed colouring. Top foliage of natural rhubarb
should be cut off leaving approximately 75mm from start of

leaf stalks. Foliage of forced rhubarb should not be cut off. Wipe stalks clean and trim off any bud scales at the bottom.

Salsify and scorzonera Roots should be clean and straight and with approximately 75mm of leaf stalk remaining.

Shallots Stage as separate bulbs and not as clusters. Bulbs should be thoroughly dried, free from staining and loose skins. Roots should be cut off to the basal plate and the tops neatly tied or whipped using uncoloured raffia. Stage on dry sand or similar material which should (preferably) be of a contrasting colour and piled on the plate slightly to raise the centre. Shallots for pickling must not exceed 30mm in diameter.

Spinach, spinach beet, chards (including white and coloured cultivars) Large, very fresh, thick, undamaged, well-coloured leaves are required. Defer gathering until the last possible moment to retain turgidity and so that there is as little delay as possible before staging. Leaves should be complete with a neatly trimmed stalk. Present in a flat fan shape overlapping the leaves. Careful handling is essential.

Squash, summer Select young, tender, shapely and uniform fruits, normally not more than five days after flowering. Fruit should be cut from the vine taking care not to mark the tender flesh. Stage as for courgettes.

Squash, winter Select fully coloured, mature fruit, with few blemishes, and of a size according to cultivar. The stalk should be retained.

Sweet corn Cobs of uniform size with fresh green husks should be displayed with approximately one quarter of the grain exposed by pulling down sharply, from the tip to the base, and removing a number of the husks. The best cobs are filled to the tip with straight rows of tender grains. The grains should be well-filled, not shrivelled. The stalks should be trimmed.

Tomatoes Select fruit of the right shape, size and colour for the cultivar. Fruit should not be overripe or with hard "green back" colouring around the calyx. Aim for a uniform firm set of fruit with firm, fresh calyces. Stage on a plate, calyx uppermost.

Turnips and swedes Select fresh, tender, disease-free roots of a size and shape according to cultivar, but not over-large and with a small tap root. Wash carefully, remove dead foliage. Cut a spare root to check inside for disease and condition.

SUGGESTIONS TO JUDGES

Judging is the exercise of deciding degrees of merit within agreed parameters. It is based on familiarity, knowledge and the insight gained from experience. It is most important that the criteria by which the subjects are to be judged are observed and abided by to the exclusion of all other considerations. Where a schedule is unclear or ambiguously worded a judge should consult the show secretary beforehand to establish exactly what is required.

1 Judging engagements Judges should seek written confirmation of all engagements. Once an engagement has been accepted, whether verbally or in writing, it is up to the judge to suggest a suitable replacement if it is found that he/she is unable to fulfil the engagement.

2 Familiarity with the schedule Before going to the show a judge should read the schedule carefully, and become familiar with any special or unusual stipulations that it contains and with all the equipment necessary to judge effectively.

3 Punctuality Anyone who has accepted an invitation to act as a judge should make every effort to reach the show at the time arranged. The organisers are naturally under an obligation to keep faith with exhibitors and the public in regard to the published time for the opening of the show and a judge who is late either reduces the already limited time for judging, delays the opening of the show, or both.

4 Time to enter the show venue As far as possible a judge should not enter the show venue until staging has been completed and exhibitors have left. He/she should not know to whom the various exhibits belong and it should be evident that a judge has avoided learning who the owners are.

5 Personal preferences and prejudices A judge must take care to see that he/she is not swayed by personal views. For example, a judge may particularly like white flowers or dislike red flowers but, if so, he/she must not give undue preference to white flowers or discount the merits of red flowers.

6 Familiarisation with the show It is advisable for judges to adjust their standards in accordance with the level of the show after consulting with the show organisers.

7 Exhibits should be judged as they are   In a competitive show the time when judging will take place is always announced beforehand and is known to the exhibitors. Exhibits should therefore be at their best at that time and should be judged as they then are. How the exhibit probably looked some time previously or how it will probably look some time later is not relevant and a judge should put such considerations out of his/her mind.

8 Speed in judging   Judges should devote to each class sufficient time to assess all the merits and detect all the faults in the exhibits. Be thorough, but not to the extent that the opening of the show is delayed as both the organisers and the public awaiting admission will be greatly inconvenienced.

9 The opinion of the majority must prevail   The judging of horticultural produce is not and never can be an exact science and a decision may often rest on something about which two opinions are tenable. When a judge believes that his/her colleagues are wrong it is his/her duty to make sure that they know his/her views but, having done that, he/she must be prepared to abide by the opinion of the majority.

10 When judges do not agree   It is desirable that the group of judges for any particular class or section should be uneven in number, three being ideal. If, as is sometimes unavoidable, the number of judges is even and they are unable to agree, they should call in the referee (if there is one) or another judge or some other competent person and abide by his/her casting vote.

11 Should exhibits be pointed?   Pointing is not necessary in order to ensure that the prizes are correctly awarded. There is usually insufficient time to point all exhibits unless there are plenty of judges. However, pointing is often helpful when assessing collection classes and other classes where there is close competition. If a class is decided by points it is recommended that this information is made available to the exhibitors and the public.

12 Procedure in judging a class   Before assessing the merits of any exhibit in a class the judges should examine the whole class and note where the exhibits in it begin and end. If the judge finds an error that can be corrected, the steward's attention should be drawn to it. All exhibits that are manifestly inferior should be dismissed from consideration and then the remainder should be compared.

In case of close competition, those exhibits in contention may be pointed. When pointing an exhibit one judge should propose the number of points under each heading and any of the other judges who does not agree with that assessment should put forward his/her own opinion. As agreement is reached on each item the figure should be noted on the judging card, so that when the points for each exhibit are totalled the figure will be one on which agreement has already been reached.

13 Collection classes   Judges should examine all the exhibits so that a true assessment of the condition and uniformity of the specimens can be made without dismantling the exhibit to such an extent that they themselves cannot reassemble the collection within the judging time.

14 Exhibits that appear to be of equal merit   It is seldom necessary or satisfactory to bracket two exhibits as equally meritorious. A careful scrutiny of exhibits that appear to be of equal merit will usually reveal something that warrants the placing of one exhibit before the other.

When there is only one award, *eg* a cup, it is essential that one exhibit should be adjudged superior to all others. If in such circumstances two exhibits obtain the same number of points, the pointing should be reviewed and, if necessary, the judges should take into consideration the arrangement of the exhibits, the relative difficulty in the cultivation of the different kinds or cultivars of which the exhibits are composed and the correctness and clearness of the labelling.

15 The withholding of prizes   If the best exhibit in a class is only worthy of the second prize, the first prize should be withheld and only the second and third prizes awarded. Similarly, if after the first prize in a class has been awarded none of the remaining exhibits is worthy of the second prize, only the third prize should be awarded.

The awarding or withholding of a prize should depend solely on the merits of the exhibits irrespective of the number of entries. Should there be only one entry in a class, if meritorious, the first prize can be awarded. Although in the interests of all concerned a standard of excellence appropriate to the show should be required, when there is doubt as to whether an exhibit is worthy of the prize offered, the exhibitor should be given the benefit of the doubt, for the object of awarding prizes is to encourage.

16 Exhibits that are "not according to schedule" As the time available for judging is seldom much more than is sufficient for the judges to decide on the relative merits of the exhibits, it is recommended that one or more stewards should be appointed to ensure, as far as possible, that all exhibits are according to schedule. But, even when stewards have been appointed, the judges are still responsible for the rejection from consideration of any exhibit that does not conform to the requirements of the schedule. The persons appointed as stewards should be competent to deal with mistakes such as too few or too many specimens and exhibits inadvertently placed in the wrong class but they cannot be expected to deal with matters that are essentially technical. The judges should write on the card of any exhibit that fails to conform to the schedule "not according to schedule". A note of the way in which the exhibit fails to conform to the schedule should be added. In exceptional circumstances it may be deemed preferable to advise the exhibitor privately, after the show, of the reason for disqualification.

When none of the exhibits in a class is according to the schedule, the prizes offered in that class should not be awarded. But if in such circumstances the exhibits are meritorious and the non-compliance with the schedule seems to be due to a misunderstanding or to an oversight or to the schedule being imperfectly worded, the judges may recommend that "special" prizes be awarded. The value of the prizes in such a case should be a matter for the committee to determine and may, if warranted, be the sums offered in the schedule. A disqualified exhibit cannot be eligible for consideration for Best in Show.

17 Any other fruit/vegetable classes When judging "any other classes" the pointing system should not be used as this is only intended for judging like against like. The criteria for judging given in *The Horticultural Show Handbook* should be followed, but a dish of a well-grown fruit or vegetable normally receiving low points should be preferred to an indifferent dish of a vegetable or fruit normally receiving high points. The question of difficulty of cultivation should only arise when there are two outstanding exhibits, one of the "low pointed" kind and one "highly pointed". In such a case the latter should be awarded the prize.

Unusual vegetables and fruits should be considered equally with those listed in "Any other class".

18 Uniform treatment of exhibits   Judges are reminded to treat all exhibits in a uniform manner. For example, in a runner bean class at least one pod in every entry should be snapped across, not only for those entries that appear to be in the running for prizes. Omission may leave an exhibitor believing that his/her exhibit has not been judged. Everything possible must be done to give the exhibitor confidence.

19 Cutting fruit or vegetables   In some circumstances judges may cut fruit or vegetables to determine the internal condition of a particular exhibit.

20 Size   Judges should remember that, whilst size is an important factor, the largest exhibit is not always the best.

21 Colour in vegetables   There are now many vegetables available in a range of colours, for example aubergines, beans, beetroot, Brussels sprouts, cauliflowers, carrots, chards, cucumbers, lettuce, onions, peppers, radishes and tomatoes. Good colour for the cultivar should be the main consideration.

22 Judging single specimens of fruit or vegetables   When only one specimen is shown, maximum points for uniformity should be included.

23 Pest infestations   Any plant with a bad pest infestation should be removed from the show bench and isolated.

THE JUDGING OF FRUITS

When assessing the relative merits of dishes of most
fruits the following features should be considered:
condition; uniformity; size; colour. A dish must consist
of one cultivar only.

Condition   Unless otherwise stated in the schedule, all fruit,
except apples, pears and gooseberries, should be ripe. Unless
the schedule states that ripe fruit is required, apples, pears and
gooseberries may be shown unripe. Nevertheless, where classes
for apples, pears or gooseberries are included in a summer
show and the schedule does not specify that the fruit must be
ripe, preference should always be given to cultivars in season
rather than to larger or more showy cultivars that have been
picked prematurely. Overripeness, shrivelling (except in gages),
malformations, absence of stalks or eyes, decay, splitting
(except in figs), blemishes due to pests or diseases, bruises or
other injury due to bad packing or any other cause and
imperfect bloom should be regarded as defects. The
preservation of the natural bloom on the surface of fruits is
greatly to be desired, not only in grapes and plums but in all
fruits, including apples and pears. All stalks and calyces should
be fresh.

Uniformity   All the specimens exhibited on a dish should be
uniform, *ie* alike in size, condition, form and colour.

Size   All fruits, except dessert apples, should be somewhat
above the average size for the cultivar but enormous
specimens should not be preferred, as beyond a certain point
size may become a defect, especially in dessert fruits. An
exhibit of a cultivar that is naturally large should not be
preferred to an exhibit of a cultivar that is naturally small,
unless the exhibit of the larger cultivar is equal or superior to
that of the smaller cultivar in other respects. In cooking (but
not dessert) apples and in all other fruits, whether dessert or
cooking, provided that the contents of two dishes are equal in
all other respects, including uniformity, the dish with the
larger specimens should be preferred. In grapes and currants,
provided that two exhibits are equal in all other respects,
including uniformity, large bunches should be preferred.

   In dessert apples, it is desirable that the fruits of the
average cultivar should not exceed 75mm in diameter, but the
judge should be aware that some cultivars are inherently

small, whereas others are naturally large, typically the triploids such as 'Jupiter' and 'Jonagold'. The judge should make due allowance for such cultivars. Nevertheless, they should not be excessively below or above the ideal size of 75mm in diameter, and it is considered that the range for dessert apples should be between 60 and 80mm in diameter. Examples of inherently small or large dessert apples are:

Small	'Margil', 'Merton Charm', 'Pitmaston Pine Apple', 'Sunset' and 'Winston'.
Large	'Belle de Boskoop', 'Blenheim Orange', 'Charles Ross', 'Mutsu' (Crispin), 'Gascoyne's Scarlet', 'Jonagold', 'Jupiter', 'Reinette du Canada', 'Rival', 'Wealthy' and 'Winter Gem'.

Dual-purpose cultivars   These are a select group of apple cultivars that are suitable both for dessert and cooking, which when shown are classified either as dessert or cooking according to their size. When the large fruits of such cultivars are shown as cooking apples they should be more than 80mm in diameter and when shown as dessert apples, they should not exceed 80mm in diameter. *(See pp64–68 for the list of dual-purpose apple cultivars, the small fruits under "Apples, dessert" and the large fruits under "Apples, cooking".)*

Colour   Attractive, naturally produced colour is meritorious but colour resulting from the removal of natural bloom or any form of polishing should be regarded as defective in any fruit.

Stalks   All fruits (except apricots, nectarines, peaches and nuts) should be shown with stalks intact. Apricots, nectarines and peaches are shown without stalks. All nuts are shown without stalks or husks.

The ripeness of fruit   Apples, pears and gooseberries may be shown either ripe or unripe and all other fruits should be ripe, unless otherwise specified in the schedule. Overripeness will be regarded as a defect in any fruit.

Glasshouse grapes   should be shown on stands unless some other method of staging is specified or permitted by the schedule.

The classification of dessert and cooking cultivars of fruits   Apples, pears and plums must be shown as dessert or cooking cultivars in accordance with the *Classified Lists* on *pp64–69* unless the schedule provides otherwise. A new cultivar not listed may be shown and if necessary a

classification as to whether it is dessert or culinary may be
obtained from the Society beforehand.

Constitution of dishes   Unless otherwise specified it is
suggested that the numbers given are used for RHS and the
leading provincial shows. Smaller shows should adopt smaller
quantities.
Number of specimens required:

Apples	6
Apricots	6
Blackberries	20
Blueberries	
dish of not less than 200g	
and not more than 250g	
Bullaces	20
Cape gooseberries	20
Cherries	20
Citrus fruits, other than kumquats and calamondins	3
Citrus fruits, kumquats and calamondins	9
Currants, black and other than black	
dish of not less than 200g	
and not more than 250g	
Damsons	20
Figs	5
Gooseberries	20
Grapes, glasshouse	1 bunch
Grapes, outdoor	2 bunches
Huckleberries	
dish of not less than 200g	
and not more than 250g	
Hybrid cane fruits *eg* boysenberries, loganberries, tayberries, sylvanberries; also Japanese wineberries	20
Kiwi fruits (Chinese gooseberries)	6
Loquats, Japanese	10
Medlars	10
Melons	1
Melons, horned (kiwanos)	2
Mulberries	20
Nectarines	5
Nuts	
dish of not less than 425g	
and not more than 450g	
Passion fruits	5
Peaches	5
Pears, including Asian pears	6
Persimmons	5
Pineapple	1
Pineapple guavas	5
Plums	9
Quinces	6
Raspberries	20
Strawberries	15
Strawberries, alpine	25
Tamarillos (tree tomatoes)	9
Worcesterberries and blackcurrant × gooseberry hybrids *eg* jostaberry	
dish of not less than 200g	
and not more than 250g	

Maximum points for a dish   The exhibition value of any kind of fruit is governed by the difficulty of producing a perfect dish *(See p11, rule 7)*. The maximum points for a perfect dish will be as follows:

	Maximum points		*Maximum points*
Apples, cooking	18	Kiwi fruits (Chinese gooseberries)	12
Apples, dessert	20	Loquats, Japanese	10
Apricots	16	Medlars	8
Blackberries	12	Melons	18
Blueberries	12	Melons, horned (kiwanos)	12
Bullaces	8	Mulberries	8
Cape gooseberries	10	Nuts	8
Cherries, sour	12	Passion fruits	12
Cherries, sweet	16	Peaches and nectarines	20
Citrus Fruits	18	Pears, Asian	18
Currants, black	12	Pears, cooking	18
Currants, other than black	12	Pears, dessert	20
Currant × gooseberry hybrids	12	Persimmons	12
Damsons	8	Pineapples	20
Figs	16	Pineapple guavas	10
Gooseberries	12	Plums, cooking	14
Grapes grown outdoors	16	Plums, dessert	16
Grapes, glasshouse	20	Quinces	12
Huckleberries	8	Raspberries	12
Hybrid cane fruits, *eg* boysenberries, loganberries, tayberries, sylvanberries; also Japanese wineberries	12	Strawberries	16
		Strawberries, alpine	8
		Tamarillos (tree tomato)	12
		Worcesterberries and blackcurrant × gooseberry hybrids	10

Alphabetical List of Fruits

Alpine strawberries
*See **Other fruits**, p63*

Apples, cooking
Merits   Large, shapely, solid fruits with undamaged eyes, stalks intact and clear unblemished skins of a colour characteristic of the cultivar.

50

Defects Fruits that are small, misshapen, overripe or soft or that have damaged eyes or lack stalks or have any blemish, including evidence of any physiological disorder such as bitter-pit or glassiness.

Condition	6 points
Uniformity	6 points
Size	6 points
TOTAL	18 points

Apples, dessert

Merits Optimum-sized shapely fruits with eyes and stalks intact and clear unblemished skins of the natural colour characteristic of the cultivar.

Defects Fruits that are too small or too large, misshapen, overripe or soft or that have damaged eyes or lack stalks or are not well coloured, or have any blemish, including evidence of any physiological disorder such as bitter-pit or glassiness.

Condition	6 points
Uniformity	6 points
Suitability of size	4 points
Colour	4 points
TOTAL	20 points

Apricots

Merits Large, highly coloured, clear-skinned, ripe fruits free from any blemish.

Defects Fruits that are small or poorly coloured or that lack clear skins or that are unripe or overripe or have any blemish.

Advice to judges For show purposes, apricots are shown without stalks

Condition	4 points
Uniformity	4 points
Size	4 points
Colour	4 points
TOTAL	16 points

Blackberries and hybrid cane fruits
eg **boysenberries, loganberries, tayberries, sylvanberries, also Japanese wineberries**

Merits   Large, ripe fruits, of good colour, free from blemishes, in good condition, with fresh calyces, and having stalks.

Defects   Fruits that are small, unripe or overripe, of a dull colour, not in good condition or that have blemishes due to insect damage or imperfect fertilisation or that lack stalks.

Advice to judges   Handle the fruit carefully, by the stalk. Take care when handling the stalks of thorny cultivars.

Condition	4 points
Uniformity	3 points
Size	3 points
Colour	2 points
TOTAL	12 points

Blueberries
Merits   Strigs with large, ripe fruits of good colour and bloom, free from blemishes, in good condition.

Defects   Fruits that are small, unripe or overripe, of a dull colour, not in good condition, blemished or with imperfect bloom, shown singly or as incomplete strigs.

Advice to judges   Handle the fruit carefully, by the strig.

Condition	4 points
Uniformity	3 points
Size	3 points
Colour	2 points
TOTAL	12 points

Boysenberries
See *Blackberries and hybrid cane fruits,* above

Bullaces
See *Damsons and bullaces, p55*

Cape gooseberries
Merits   Calyces intact, dry, ochre-coloured, clean, blemish-free containing large ripe, unblemished fruits of good colour.

Defects   Calyces immature, damaged, blemished, containing small or under-ripe or overripe fruits of poor colour or condition.

Advice to judges   Open the calyces of one or more specimen in each exhibit to ensure the fruit is in good condition and of reasonable size.

Condition	4 points
Uniformity	2 points
Size	2 points
Colour	2 points
TOTAL	10 points

Cherries, sour

Merits   Large, ripe fruits, of brilliant colour, with unshrivelled stalks.

Defects   Fruits that are small, unripe or overripe, of dull colour or that are splitting or have any blemish or that lack stalks or have shrivelled stalks.

Advice to judges   Handle the fruit carefully, by the stalk.

Condition	3 points
Uniformity	3 points
Size	3 points
Colour	3 points
TOTAL	12 points

Cherries, sweet

Merits   Large, ripe fruits, of brilliant colour, with unshrivelled stalks.

Defects   Fruits that are small, unripe or overripe, of dull colour or that are splitting or have any blemish or that lack stalks or have shrivelled stalks.

Advice to judges   Handle the fruit carefully, by the stalk.

Condition	4 points
Uniformity	4 points
Size	4 points
Colour	4 points
TOTAL	16 points

Citrus fruits

Merits   Large, shapely ripe fruits of good even colour natural to the cultivar with bright, shiny unblemished skins.

Defects   Fruits that are small, misshapen, unripe or overripe of dull or uneven colour or have any blemish.

Condition	5 points
Uniformity	5 points
Size	4 points
Colour	4 points
TOTAL	18 points

Currants, black

Merits Strigs with full complement of berries. Berries large, ripe and of a uniform, bright, jet-black colour. Stalks fresh.

Defects Strigs without full complement of berries. Berries small, unripe or overripe or unevenly ripened or of a dull colour or having shrivelled stalks.

Advice to judges Some modern cultivars, such as 'Ben Connan', 'Ben Hope', 'Ben Loyal' and 'Ben Sarek' do not produce long strigs. In the case of these cultivars, a small part of the woody stem is permissible. Handle the fruit carefully, by the strig.

Condition	3 points
Uniformity	3 points
Size	3 points
Colour	3 points
TOTAL	12 points

Currants, other than black

Merits Strigs with full complement of berries. Berries large, ripe and of a uniform, brilliant colour. Stalks fresh.

Defects Strigs without full complement of berries. Berries small, unripe or overripe or unevenly ripened or of a dull colour or having shrivelled stalks.

Advice to judges Handle the fruit carefully, by the strig.

Condition	3 points
Uniformity	3 points
Size	3 points
Colour	3 points
TOTAL	12 points

Currant × gooseberry hybrids
eg jostaberry, also worcesterberry

Merits Strigs with full complement of berries. Berries large, ripe, uniform and of even colour. Stalks fresh.

Defects Strigs without full complement of berries. Berries small, unripe or overripe, of poor or uneven colour, diseased or blemished or having shrivelled stalks.

Advice to judges Handle the fruit carefully, by the strig.

Condition	3 points
Uniformity	3 points
Size	3 points
Colour	3 points
TOTAL	12 points

Damsons and bullaces

All damsons and bullaces rank as cooking fruits.

Merits   Large, ripe but firm fruits, of good colour, carrying perfect bloom and having stalks.

Defects   Fruits small, unripe or so ripe as to be soft, of poor colour or with imperfect bloom or lacking stalks.

Condition	2 points
Uniformity	2 points
Size	2 points
Colour	2 points
TOTAL	8 points

Figs

Merits   Large, fully ripe fruits, of good colour with bloom and stalks intact.

Defects   Fruits small, unripe, of poor colour or with imperfect bloom.

Advice to judges   Slight splitting is not a defect

Condition	5 points
Uniformity	3 points
Size	5 points
Colour	3 points
TOTAL	16 points

Gages

*See **Plums, dessert, and gages**, p61*

Gooseberries

Merits   Large, ripe or unripe fruits as appropriate for the season, uniform and unblemished, of good colour, complete with stalks.

Defects   Fruits small, uneven, overripe, diseased, blemished, of poor colour or lacking stalks.

Condition	4 points
Uniformity	3 points
Size	3 points
Colour	2 points
TOTAL	12 points

Grapes (glasshouse dessert)

Merits Large complete bunches, although large bunches of a poor quality are not so meritorious as smaller ones of a good quality. Symmetrical, complete, well-balanced bunches, of uniform size and shape and properly thinned so that each berry has had room to develop.

Large berries, of uniform size, good colour, fully ripe and well finished with a dense, intact bloom.

Defects Bunches that are small, ill balanced, lacking uniformity in size or shape or that are loose or so crowded that some berries have not had room to develop properly. Berries that are small, lacking in uniformity, of poor colour or not fully ripe and poorly finished or overripe, diseased or that have little or only imperfect bloom or have withered stems or have spots or blemishes of any sort.

Advice to judges The fruit should be shown with a piece of lateral shoot on either side of the stalk to form a T-handle. Judges should take into account the extra skill in growing the more exacting cultivars 'Muscat of Alexandria', 'Canon Hall Muscat', 'Muscat Hamburgh', Madresfield Court', 'Mrs Pearson', 'Mrs Pince' or 'Prince of Wales'.

Condition	5 points
Colour	5 points
Size, shape and density of bunch	5 points
Size and uniformity of berry	5 points
TOTAL	20 points

Grapes (grown outdoors for wine or dessert)

Merits Large, complete, well-filled and balanced bunches carrying large berries, unblemished, typical of the cultivar, of uniform size, good colour, fully ripe and well finished with a dense intact bloom.

Defects Bunches that are small, underdeveloped or lacking uniformity. Berries that are blemished, rotting, split, have withered stems, unripe or overripe, poorly finished or with little or imperfect bloom.

Advice to judges

Condition	4 points
Size and uniformity of berry	4 points
Size, shape and density of bunch	4 points
Colour	4 points
TOTAL	16 points

Huckleberries
See Other fruits, p63

Japanese loquats
See Other fruits, p63

Japanese wineberries
See Blackberries and hybrid cane fruits, p52

Jostaberries
See Currant × gooseberry hybrids, p54

Kiwi fruits (Chinese gooseberries)
Merits   Large, ripe fruits, evenly shaped and uniform, with unblemished skins and stalks intact.
Defects   Fruits that are small, unripe or are uneven, lack uniformity or have any blemish or are without stalks.

Condition	4 points
Uniformity	4 points
Size	4 points
TOTAL	12 points

Loganberries
See Blackberries and hybrid cane fruits, p52

Medlars
Merits   Fruits that are ripe with clean skins, stalks intact and of a size according to cultivar.
Defects   Fruits that are unripe, small for the cultivar or have blotched skins.

Condition	3 points
Uniformity	3 points
Size	2 points
TOTAL	8 points

Melons

Merits   A large fruit (for the cultivar), clean, shapely, free from blemishes, fully ripe and well finished.

Defects   A small fruit (for the cultivar), or one that is unripe or overripe or is blemished or misshapen.

Advice to judges   Gently press the skin of a melon, which should "give" a little when ripe, and there should be a slight aroma. The fruit should be shown with a piece of lateral shoot on either side of the stalk to form a T-handle.

Condition	6 points
Size	6 points
Colour and finish	6 points
TOTAL	18 points

Melons, horned (kiwanos)

Merits   Large, ripe fruits, clean, firm, of uniform golden or orange colour; blemish-free and well finished.

Defects   Small, unripe fruits, damaged or of poor colour, lacking firmness, or overripe.

Advice to judges   The fruit should be shown with a piece of lateral shoot on either side of the stalk to form a T-handle.

Condition	4 points
Size	4 points
Colour and finish	4 points
TOTAL	12 points

Mulberries

Merits   Large, ripe fruits of good colour, free from blemishes and in excellent condition.

Defects   Fruits that are small, unripe or overripe, of a dull colour, not in good condition, imperfectly formed or have blemishes.

Condition	2 points
Uniformity	2 points
Size	2 points
Colour	2 points
TOTAL	8 points

Nectarines

See **Peaches and nectarines**, *p59*

Nuts

Merits Large nuts with clean shells and plump kernels filling the cavities. In walnuts, nuts that are well sealed with thin shells.

Defects Nuts that are small, or have spotted shells or shrivelled kernels or kernels that do not fill the shells or are unsound. In walnuts, nuts that are poorly sealed or have shells that are not thin.

Advice to judges Nuts are shown without stalks or husks. One specimen from each exhibit should be opened to ensure the kernel is full.

Condition	2 points
Uniformity	3 points
Size	3 points
TOTAL	8 points

Passion fruits

See Other fruits, p63

Peaches and nectarines

Merits Large fruits (for the cultivar), fully ripe with the colour natural to the cultivar well developed, free from bruises and other blemishes.

Defects Fruits that are small (for the cultivar), unripe or overripe with colour not well developed, or bruised or with any other blemish.

Advice to judges For show purposes, peaches and nectarines are shown without stalks

Condition	5 points
Uniformity	5 points
Size	5 points
Colour	5 points
TOTAL	20 points

Pears, Asian

Merits   Large, shapely fruits with undamaged eyes, stalks intact, of good colour and with unblemished clear or finely russeted skins characteristic of the cultivar.

Defects   Fruits that are small, misshapen or shrivelled, or lack stalks or of poor colour or have any blemish.

Condition	5 points
Uniformity	5 points
Size	4 points
Colour	4 points
TOTAL	18 points

Pears, cooking

Refer to Classified List of Fruits, p68, for the list of cultivars

Merits   Large (for the cultivar), shapely fruits with undamaged eyes, stalks intact and clear, unblemished skins of a colour characteristic of the cultivar.

Defects   Fruits that are small for the cultivar, misshapen, overripe or soft or that have damaged eyes or lack stalks or have any blemish.

Advice to judges   Only those pears listed as cooking pears on *p68* can be accepted as cooking pears.

Condition	6 points
Uniformity	6 points
Size	6 points
TOTAL	18 points

Pears, dessert

Merits   Large for the cultivar, shapely fruits with undamaged eyes, stalks intact and clear, unblemished skins of the natural colour characteristic of the cultivar.

Defects   Fruits that are small, misshapen or shrivelled or that have damaged eyes or lack stalks or are not well coloured or have any blemish.

Condition	6 points
Uniformity	6 points
Size	4 points
Colour	4 points
TOTAL	20 points

Persimmons

*See **Other fruits**, p63*

Pineapple guavas
See Other fruits, p63

Pineapples
Merits A fruit that is large for the cultivar, ripe and of a golden colour throughout, shapely, with segments of even size, free from blemish and having a fresh-looking crown that is in proportion to the fruit, *ie* about half its length.

Defects A fruit that is small for the cultivar, not fully ripe or overripe, of uneven shape, having poorly formed segments due to imperfect fertilisation, showing insect damage, having a crown that is not fresh or is not in proportion to the fruit.

Condition	10 points
Size	6 points
Colour	4 points
TOTAL	20 points

Plums, cooking
Merits Large, firm, ripe fruits, of good colour, carrying perfect bloom, and having stalks.

Defects Fruits that are small, unripe or so ripe as to be soft, of poor colour or with imperfect bloom or lacking stalks.

Advice to judges Handle the fruit carefully, by the stalk.

Condition	4 points
Uniformity	3 points
Size	4 points
Colour	3 points
TOTAL	14 points

Plums, dessert, and gages
Merits Large, fully ripe fruits, of good colour, with bloom intact and having stalks.

Defects Fruits that are small, unripe or overripe, of poor colour, with imperfect bloom or lacking stalks.

Advice to judges Handle the fruit carefully, by the stalk. Slight shrivelling in gages is not a defect.

Condition	5 points
Uniformity	4 points
Size	3 points
Colour	4 points
TOTAL	16 points

Quinces

Merits   Large, shapely fruits with eyes and stalks intact and unblemished skins.

Defects   Fruits that are small or misshapen or have damaged eyes or lack stalks or have any blemish.

Condition	4 points
Uniformity	4 points
Size	4 points
TOTAL	12 points

Raspberries

Merits   Large, ripe fruits, of good colour, free from blemishes, in good condition, with fresh calyces, and having stalks.

Defects   Fruits that are small, unripe or overripe, of a dull colour, not in good condition or have blemishes due to insect damage or imperfect fertilisation or that lack stalks.

Advice to judges   Handle the fruit carefully, by the stalk.

Condition	4 points
Uniformity	2 points
Size	3 points
Colour	3 points
TOTAL	12 points

Strawberries

Merits   Large, ripe fruits, of good colour, bright and fresh, free from blemish, in good condition, with fresh calyces, and having stalks.

Defects   Fruits that are small, unripe or overripe, of a dull colour, not in good condition or that are "hard-nosed" through imperfect fertilisation or lacking stalks.

Advice to judges   Handle the fruit carefully, by the stalk.

Condition	4 points
Uniformity	4 points
Size	4 points
Colour	4 points
TOTAL	16 points

Strawberries, alpine

See Other fruits, p63

Sylvanberries

See Blackberries and hybrid cane fruits, p52

Tayberries
See **Blackberries and hybrid cane fruits**, *p52*

Worcesterberries
See **Currant × gooseberry hybrids**, *p54*

Other fruits
This is a category to cover fruits not usually seen on the show
bench but which may occur from time to time, including the
kinds that for various reasons are enjoying a degree of
popularity. Some of the fruits may eventually become more
widely grown and warrant being listed in their own right
whereas others may fade into obscurity. Fruits considered to be
in this category at present are listed below, each with a
recommended points value. The considerations of condition,
size, colour and uniformity will apply.

Garden huckleberry (*Solanum melanocerasum*)	8 points
Huckleberry (*Gaylussacia baccata*)	8 points
Japanese loquat (*Eriobotrya japonica*)	10 points
Passion fruit (*Passiflora* species)	12 points
Persimmon (*Diospyros kaki*)	12 points
Pineapple guava (*Acca sellowiana*)	10 points
Strawberries, alpine	8 points
Tamarillo or tree tomato (*Cyphomandra betacea*)	12 points

Classified List of Fruits

For exhibition purposes it is necessary to distinguish between dessert and cooking cultivars of apples, pears and plums and the following lists are drawn up for this purpose alone. These must be exhibited as dessert or cooking cultivars in accordance with these lists. The apples denoted as either small or large are classified as dual-purpose fruits. *(See p48, Dual-purpose cultivars.)*
Asterisks (*) indicate russet cultivars of dessert apples.

Apples, dessert

'Acme'
'Adams's Pearmain'
'Alkmene' (Early Windsor)
'Allen's Everlasting'*
'Allington Pippin'
Ambassy ('Dalil')
'American Mother'
'Ard Cairn Russet'*
'Aromatic Russet'*
'Ashmead's Kernel'*
'Autumn Pearmain'
'Baker's Delicious'
'Baldwin'
'Bardsey'
'Barnack Beauty'
'Barnack Orange'
'Baumann's Reinette'
'Beauty of Bath'
'Beauty of Bedford'
'Beauty of Hants', small fruits
'Belle de Boskoop', small fruits
'Ben's Red'
'Bess Pool'
'Blenheim Orange', small fruits
'Bloody Ploughman'
'Bolero'
'Braddick's Nonpareil'
'Braeburn'
'Brownlee's Russet'*
'Calville Blanc d'Hiver'
'Captain Kidd'

'Charles Ross', small fruits
'Cheddar Cross'
'Cherry Cox' (sport of 'Cox's Orange Pippin')
'Chivers' Delight'
'Christmas Pearmain'
'Claygate Pearmain'
'Cockle Pippin'*
'Colonel Vaughan' ('Kentish Pippin')
'Cornish Aromatic'
'Cornish Gilliflower'
'Cortland'
'Coronation'
'Court Pendu Plat'
'Cox's Orange Pippin'
'Crimson Cox' (sport of 'Cox's Orange Pippin')
'Crowngold' (sport of 'Jonagold')
'Cutler Grieve'
Cybèle ('Delrouval')
'D'Arcy Spice'*
'Delcorf' (Delbarestivale)
'Delgollune' (Delbard Jubilé)
'Delicious'
'Devonshire Quarrenden'
'Discovery'
'Duchess's Favourite'
'Duke of Devonshire'*
'Easter Orange'
'Egremont Russet'*
'Ellison's Orange'
'Elstar'

'Empire'
'Exeter Cross'
'Falstaff'
'Fearn's Pippin'
'Fiesta' (Red Pippin)
'Flamenco'
'Fuji'
'Gala'
'Gascoyne's Scarlet', small
   fruits
'Gavin'
'George Carpenter'
'George Cave'
'Gladstone'
'Gloster 69'
'Golden Delicious'
'Golden Reinette'
'Golden Russet'*
'Goldilocks'
'Granny Smith'
'Gravenstein'
'Greensleeves'
'Grimes Golden'
'Herefordshire Russet'
'Heusgen's Golden Reinette'
'High View Pippin'
'Hitchin Pippin'
'Holstein'
'Houblon'
'Hubbard's Pearmain'
'Idared'
'Ingrid Marie'
'Irish Peach'
'James Grieve'
'Jerseymac'
'Jester'
'Joaneting' (white)
'John Standish'
'Jonagold'
'Jonagored' (sport of
   'Jonagold')
'Jonathan'
'Joybells'
'Jumbo', small fruits
'Jupiter'
'Karmijn de Sonnaville'
'Katja' (Katy)

'Kent'
'Kerry Pippin'
'Kidd's Orange Red'
'King George V'
'King of the Pippins'
'King Russet'* (sport of 'King
   of the Pippins')
'King's Acre Pippin'
'Lady Sudeley'
'Landsberger Reinette'
'Langley Pippin'
'Laxton's Advance'
'Laxton's Early Crimson'
'Laxton's Epicure'
'Laxton's Exquisite'
'Laxton's Fortune'
'Laxton's Pearmain'
'Laxton's Superb'
'Limelight'
'Lord Burghley'
'Lord Hindlip'
'Lord Lambourne'
'Mabbott's Pearmain'
'McIntosh Red'
'Madresfield Court'
'Maidstone Favourite'
'Mannington's Pearmain'
'Margaret' ('Red Joaneting')
'Margil'
'May Queen'
'Melba'
'Meridian'
'Melrose'
'Merton Beauty'
'Merton Charm'
'Merton Joy'
'Merton Knave'
'Merton Prolific'
'Merton Russet'*
'Merton Worcester'
'Michaelmas Red'
'Miller's Seeding'
'Millicent Barnes'
'Mutsu' (Crispin), small fruits
'Nanny'
'Newtown Pippin'
'Nonpareil'*

'Norfolk Royal'
'Norfolk Royal Russet'* (sport
  of 'Norfolk Royal Russet')
'Northern Spy'
'Nutmeg Pippin'*
'Orleans Reinette'
'Owen Thomas'
'Park Farm Pippin'
'Paroquet'
'Pearl'
'Pine Golden Pippin'*
'Pineapple Russet'*
'Pinova'
'Pitmaston Russet Nonpareil'*
'Pitmaston Pine Apple'*
'Pixie'
Polka ('Trajan')
'Queen Cox' (sport of 'Cox's
  Orange Pippin')
'Red Astrachan'
'Red Delicious'
'Red Devil'
'Red Ellison'
'Red Juneating'
'Red Melba'
'Red Pixie'
'Redsleeves'
Regali ('Delkistar')
'Reinette du Canada'*
'Reinette Rouge Etoilée'
  ('Calville Rouge Précoce')
'Renown'
'Ribston Pippin'
'Rival'
'Rosemary Russet'*
'Ross Nonpareil'
'Roundway Magnum
  Bonum', small fruits
'Roxbury Russet' ('Boston
  Russet')*
'Royal Gala' ('Tenroy')
'Rubinette'
'Rushock Pearmain'
'Saint Cecilia'
'Saint Edmund's Pippin'*
  ('Saint Edmund's Russet'*)
'Saint Everard'

'Saltcote Pippin'
'Sanspareil'
'Saturn'
'Scarlet Nonpareil'
'Scrumptious'
'Siddington Russet'*
'Sir John Thornycroft'
'Smoothee'
'Spartan'
'Stark's Earliest'
'Star of Devon'
'Sturmer Pippin'
'Summerred'
'Summer Golden Pippin'
'Sunrise'
'Sunset'
'Suntan'
'Sweet Society'
'Syke House Russet'*
'Telstar'
Tentation ('Delblush')
'Tydeman's Early Worcester'
'Tydeman's Late Orange'
'Vistabella'
'Wagener'
'Waltz'
'Wealthy'
'Wheeler's Russet'*
'White Astrachan'
'White Transparent'
'William Crump'
'William's Favourite'*
'Winston'
'Winter Banana'
'Winter Gem'
'Winter Queening'
'Woolbrook Pippin'
'Worcester Pearmain'
'Wyken Pippin'*
'Yellow Ingestrie'
'Zabergau Reinette*

Apples, cooking

'Arthur W. Barnes'
'Alfriston'
'Annie Elizabeth'
'Arthur Turner'
'Beauty of Hants', large fruits
'Beauty of Kent'
'Belle de Boskoop', large fruits
'Belle de Pontoise'
'Bess Pool'
'Bismarck'
'Blenheim Orange', large fruits
'Bountiful'
'Bow Hill Pippin'
'Bramley's Seedling'
'Broad Eyed Pippin'
'Broadholm Beauty'
'Bushey Grove'
'Burr Knot'
'Byford Wonder'
'Carlisle Codlin'
'Catshead'
'Cellini'
'Charles Eyre'
'Charles Ross', large fruits
'Charlotte'
'Chelmsford Wonder'
'Cottenham Seedling'
'Cox's Pomona'
'Crawley Beauty'
'Crimson Bramley' (sport of 'Bramley's Seedling')
'Crimson Peasgood' (sport of 'Peasgood's Nonsuch')
'Dewdney's Seedling' ('Baron Wolseley')
'Duchess of Oldenburg'
'Dummellor's Seedling' ('Dumelow's Seedling', 'Wellington', 'Normanton Wonder')
'Ecklinville'
'Edward VII'
'Emneth Early' ('Early Victoria')

'Emperor Alexander'
'Encore'
'French Crab'
'Galloway Pippin'
'Gascoyne's Scarlet', large fruits
'George Neal'
'Gloria Mundi'
'Golden Noble'
'Golden Spire'
'Gooseberry'
'Grenadier'
'Hambledon Deux Ans'
'Hambling's Seedling'
'Harvey'
'Hawthornden'
'Herefordshire Beefing'
'Herring's Pippin', large fruits
'Hoary Morning'
'Hollandbury'
'Hormead Pearmain'
'Howgate Wonder'
'John Waterer'
'Jumbo', large fruits
'Kentish Fillbasket'
'Keswick Codlin'
'King's Acre Bountiful'
'Lady Henniker'
'Lane's Prince Albert'
'Lemon Pippin'
'Lewis' Incomparable'
'Loddington' ('Stone's')
'Lodi'
'Lord Derby'
'Lord Grosvenor'
'Lord Stradbroke'
'Lord Suffield'
'Mere de Menage'
'Monarch'
'Mutsu' (Crispin), large fruits
'Nancy Jackson'
'New Bess Pool'
'New Hawthornden'
'New Northern Greening'
'Newton Wonder'

'Norfolk Beauty'
'Norfolk Beefing'
'Northern Greening'
'Ontario'
'Peasgood's Nonsuch'
'Pott's Seedling'
'Queen'
'Red Victoria'
'Reverend W.Wilks'
'Rhode Island Greening'
'Roundway Magnum
   Bonum', large fruits
'Royal Jubilee'
'Royal Late'
'Royal Russet'

'Sandringham'
'Schoolmaster'
'Shoesmith'
'Sowman's Seedling'
'Stirling Castle'
'Striped Beefing'
'S.T.Wright'
'Tom Putt'
'Thomas Rivers'
'Tower of Glamis'
'Twenty Ounce'
'Upton Pyne'
'Waltham Abbey Seedling'
'Warner's King'
'Woolbrook Russet'

Damsons, including bullaces

All damsons and bullaces rank as cooking fruits.

Pears

The following are classified as cooking pears at RHS Shows:

'Beurré Clairgeau'
'Black Worcester'
'Catillac'

'Uvedale's St Germain'
'Vicar of Winkfield'

Plums, dessert

'Angelina Burdett'
'Anna Spath'
'Ariel'
'Avalon'
'Blue Rock'
'Blue Tit'
'Bryanston Gage'
'Coe's Golden Drop'
'Count Althann's Gage'
'Cox's Emperor'
'Crimson Drop'
'Drap d'or d'Esperen'
'Edda'
'Excalibur'
Gages, all cultivars
'Goldfinch'
'Grove's Late Victoria'
'Herman'
'Imperial Gage' ('Denniston's Superb')
'Jefferson'
'Jubilaeum'
'Kirke's'
'Laxton's Delight'
'Laxton's Gage'
'Merton Gem'
'Monsieur Hatiff' ('Red Gage')
'Ontario'
'Opal'
'Oullin's Golden'
'Reeves Seedling'
'Reine-Claude Dorée'
'Sanctus Hubertus'
'Seneca'
'Severn Cross'
'Thames Cross'
'Utility'
'Valerie'
'Valor'
'Victoria'
'Victory'
'Violetta'
'Washington'

Plums, cooking

'Autumn Compote'
'Belgian Purple'
'Belle de Louvain'
'Blaisdon Red'
'Curlew'
'Czar'
'Diamond'
'Early Laxton'
'Edwards'
'Giant Prune'
'Guinevere'
'Heron'
'Laxton's Cropper'
'Marjorie's Seedling'
'Mirabelle', all cultivars
'Monarch'
'Myrobalan'
'Orleans'
'Pershore'
'Pond's Seedling'
'President'
'Purple Pershore'
'Warwickshire Drooper'
'White Magnum Bonum'
'Wyedale'

THE JUDGING OF VEGETABLES

In assessing the merits of exhibits of vegetables the following features should usually be considered: condition, uniformity, size, colour.

A dish must consist of one cultivar only.

Condition Cleanliness, freshness, tenderness and presence or absence of coarseness and blemishes.

Uniformity The state of being alike in size, shape, condition and colour. When only one specimen is shown and points for uniformity are available, those points should be included.

Size This is meritorious if accompanied by quality (but only in those circumstances) as the production of large specimens of good quality requires more skill than the production of small specimens. The size of vegetable most suitable for table use varies with the consumer.

Colour This should reflect freshness, trueness to cultivar and maturity.

Constitution of dishes Unless otherwise specified it is suggested that the numbers given are used for RHS and the leading provincial shows. Smaller shows should adopt smaller quantities.

Number of specimens required:	in collections	for single dishes
Artichokes, globe	3	2
Artichokes, Jerusalem	6	6
Asparagus	12	6
Asparagus peas	18 *pods*	12 *pods*
Aubergines	3	3
Beans, broad	12	9
Beans, French	12	9
Beans, runner	12	9
Beetroot, cylindrical, globe	6	4
Beetroot, long	3	3
Broccoli, coloured-headed	3	2
Broccoli, sprouting (shoots)	12	12

Judging of Vegetables

Number of specimens required:	in collections	for single dishes
Brussels sprouts	20	15
Cabbages, Chinese*	3	2
Cabbages, green, red, Savoy*	3	2
Calabrese (heads**)	3	2
Carrots, long pointed	3	3
Carrots, stump rooted	6	3
Cauliflowers*	3	2
Celeriac	4	2
Celery	4	2
Chicory, chicons	6	3
Chicory, other types	3	2
Chives	1 *bunch***	1 *bunch***
Corn salad (lambs' lettuce)	1 *dish of 12 plants*	1 *dish of 9 plants*
Courgettes	4	3
Cress (seedlings)	****	****
Cress, American or land	1 *bunch of 12 plants*	1 *bunch of 9 plants*
Cucumbers	3	2
Endive, all types	3	2
Fennel, Florence	3	2
Garlic	6 *bulbs*	5 *bulbs*
Herbs	1 *bunch***	1 *bunch***
Kale (leaves)	10	10
Kohlrabi	4	3
Leeks	4	3
Leeks (pot)	4	2
Lettuces, all types	3	2
Marrows	2	2
Mushrooms	12	12
Mustard or rape (seedlings)	****	****
Okra	4	3
Onions, over 250g	6	3
Onions, 250g or under	6	5
Onions, green salad	12	12
Onions, pickling	12	12
Oriental brassicas (flower stalks)	12	12
Oriental brassicas (heading types)	3	2
Oriental brassicas (loose-leaved types)	3	2
Parsnips	3	3
Peas	12 *pods*	9 *pods*

Judging of Vegetables

Number of specimens required:	in collections	for single dishes
Peppers, hot (chilli)	6	6
Peppers, sweet	6	3
Potatoes	6	5
Pumpkin	1	1
Radishes, Oriental, winter	3	3
Radishes, small salad	12	9
Rhubarb, forced	6 *sticks*	3 *sticks*
Rhubarb, natural	6 *sticks*	3 *sticks*
Salading vegetables, miscellaneous	3	2
Salsify	3	2
Scorzonera	3	2
Seakale (heads)	3	2
Shallots	12	12
Spinach, spinach beet, chards	15 *leaves*	15 *leaves*
Spinach, New Zealand	15 *tips*	15 *tips*
Squash, summer	4	3
Squash, winter	1	1
Swedes	3	2
Sweet corn	3	3
Tomatoes, large	6	3
Tomatoes, medium	9	9
Tomatoes, small	15	15
Turnips	6	3
Watercress	3 *bunches****	1 *bunch****

* Cabbages and cauliflowers may be shown without stalks in collection classes only.

** Calabrese sideshoots should be exhibited as broccoli, sprouting.

*** Chives, watercress or any herb should be sufficient to fill a vase approximately 150mm high and 65mm at the mouth.

**** Mustard and cress should be exhibited in growth, not cut and be shown in not less than two 150mm pans or their equivalent. If both mustard and cress are shown they will count as one item. Either may be shown alone. Rape will count as mustard.

Maximum points for a dish The exhibition value of any kind of vegetable is governed by the difficulty of producing a perfect dish *(see p11, rule 7)*. The maximum points for a perfect dish will be as follows:

	maximum points		maximum points
Artichokes, globe	15	Fennel, Florence	15
Artichokes, Jerusalem	10	Fruiting vegetables, miscellaneous	12
Asparagus	15		
Asparagus peas	12	Garlic	15
Aubergines	18	Herbs	10
Beans, broad	15	Kale, curly (borecole)	12
Beans, French	15	Kohlrabi	12
Beans, runner	18	Leaf vegetables, miscellaneous	10
Beetroot, cylindrical, globe	15		
Beetroot, long	20	Leeks (blanched or intermediate)	20
Broccoli, coloured-headed	18		
Broccoli, sprouting	15	Leeks (pot)	20
Brussels sprouts	15	Lettuce, butterhead, cos or crisp	15
Cabbages, Chinese	15		
Cabbages, green	15	Lettuce, loose-leaf	12
Cabbages, red	15	Marrows	15
Cabbages, Savoy	15	Mushrooms	15
Calabrese	15	Mustard or rape	10
Carrots, long pointed	20	Okra	18
Carrots, stump rooted	18	Onions, exhibition, over 250g	20
Cauliflowers	20		
Celeriac	15	Onions 250g or under	15
Celery, blanched or trench	20	Onions, green salad	12
		Onions, pickling	12
Celery, self-blanching or green	18	Oriental brassicas, flowering stalks	15
Chards	12	Oriental brassicas, heading	15
Chicory, chicons or other types	15	Oriental brassicas, loose-leaf or rosette	12
Chives	10		
Corn salad (lambs' lettuce)	10	Parsnips	20
		Peas	20
Courgettes	12	Peas, mangetout or snap	15
Cress	10	Peppers, hot (chilli) or sweet	15
Cress, American or land	10		
Cucumbers, under protection	18	Potatoes	20
		Pumpkins	10
Cucumbers, outdoor grown	15	Radishes, Oriental or winter	15
Dandelion, blanched	10	Radishes, small salad	10
Endive	15	Rhubarb, forced	15

	maximum points		maximum points
Rhubarb, natural	12	Spinach, New Zealand	12
Root vegetables, miscellaneous	15	Squash, summer	12
		Squash, winter	10
Salading vegetables, miscellaneous	10	Swedes	15
		Sweet corn	18
Salsify	15	Tomatoes, large	15
Scorzonera	15	Tomatoes, medium	18
Seakale	15	Tomatoes, small	12
Shallots, exhibition	18	Turnips	15
Shallots, pickling	15	Watercress	10
Spinach or spinach beet	12		

Alphabetical list of vegetables

Artichokes, globe

Merits   Large, heavy, shapely, well-closed heads of plump, solid fleshy scales.

Defects   Heads that are small, lightweight, irregular or loose, or that have thin or shrivelled scales.

Advice to judges   Look for well-grown specimens with symmetrical heads and closely-knit scales.

Condition	5 points
Uniformity	3 points
Size	2 points
Shape	2 points
Colour	3 points
TOTAL	15 points

Artichokes, Jerusalem

Merits   Shapely, large tubers with smooth, unblemished skins.

Defects   Tubers of very irregular shape, or that are small or have rough or patchy skins.

Advice to judges   *See Merits and Defects above*

Condition	4 points
Uniformity	2 points
Size	2 points
Shape	2 points
TOTAL	10 points

Asparagus

Merits Fresh, long, straight, plump, dark green stems with well-closed scales.
Defects Stems that are short, crooked, thin, shrivelled or dull-coloured or that have open scales.
Advice to judges *See Merits and Defects above*

Condition	5 points
Uniformity	3 points
Size	3 points
Shape	2 points
Colour	2 points
TOTAL	15 points

Asparagus peas

Merits Well-shaped tender unblemished pods, approximately 30–40mm long with stalks attached.
Defects Misshapen, damaged pods that are tough or immature or that lack stalks.
Advice to judges Snap a pod from each exhibit to check for condition of inner fibrous layer.

Condition	4 points
Uniformity	3 points
Size of pods	3 points
Colour	2 points
TOTAL	12 points

Aubergines

Merits Large, shapely, solid, bright, well-coloured fruits free from blemishes and with fresh calyces.
Defects Fruits that are small, misshapen, shrivelled, dull or poorly coloured.
Advice to judges Fruits should be firm and of good shape with natural bloom and fresh calyces.

Condition	5 points
Uniformity	4 points
Size	3 points
Shape	3 points
Colour	3 points
TOTAL	18 points

Beans, broad

Merits   Long, fresh, well-filled pods with stalks and clear unblemished skins and tender seeds of good size.

Defects   Short pods that are small, not fresh or that are blemished, imperfectly filled or contain seeds that are not tender.

Advice to judges   Choose long, blemish-free pods. Open one pod from each exhibit. Seeds should not be split, have black hilums ("eyes"), be detached from the pod or show evidence of pest damage.

Condition	5 points
Uniformity	3 points
Size	3 points
Shape	2 points
Colour	2 points
TOTAL	15 points

Beans, climbing, other than runner
See Beans, French, below

Beans, French

Merits   Straight, fresh, tendersnap pods with stalks, and of even length and good colour with no outward sign of seeds.

Defects   Pods that are misshapen, dull, pale, shrivelled, tough, stringy or that have prominent seeds.

Advice to judges   Snap one pod from each exhibit to determine freshness.

Condition	5 points
Uniformity	3 points
Size	3 points
Shape	2 points
Colour	2 points
TOTAL	15 points

Beans, runner

Merits   Long, uniform, straight, shapely, fresh pods of good colour with stalks, uniform tails and no outward sign of seeds.
Defects   Pods that are short, misshapen, damaged or bottle-necked and when snapped are stringy, limp or show prominent seeds.
Advice to judges   Snap one pod from each exhibit to determine freshness.

Condition	5 points
Uniformity	4 points
Size	3 points
Shape	4 points
Colour	2 points
TOTAL	18 points

Beetroot, cylindrical

Merits   Well proportioned, of approximately 150mm in length, with a taproot and smooth skin of a uniform dark colour. Foliage trimmed to approximately 75mm.
Defects   Specimens that are too large, too small, misshapen, tough, multi-rooted, or are marked with pest damage, have rough corky skin, or show signs of age.
Advice to judges   Look for specimens uniform in size, shape and colour with clean, firm, damage-free skin with a single taproot and foliage trimmed to approximately 75mm.

Condition	5 points
Uniformity	3 points
Size	2 points
Shape	3 points
Colour	2 points
TOTAL	15 points

Beetroot, globe red

Merits   Spherical, of approximately 60–75mm in diameter with a taproot and smooth skin of a uniform dark colour. Foliage trimmed to approximately 75mm.

Defects   Specimens that are too large, too small, misshapen, tough, multi-rooted, or are marked with pest damage, have rough corky skin, or show signs of age.

Advice to judges   Look for specimens uniform in size, shape and colour with clean, firm, damage-free skin with a single taproot and foliage trimmed to approximately 75mm.

Condition	5 points
Uniformity	3 points
Size	2 points
Shape	3 points
Colour	2 points
TOTAL	15 points

Beetroot, globe, other than red

*See **Beetroot, globe red**, above (except that colour should be according to the cultivar.)*

Beetroot, long

Merits   Long, firm well-shaped roots, evenly tapered, with clean, broad shoulders, of a uniform colour and free from side-shoots. Foliage trimmed to approximately 75mm.

Defects   Specimens that are misshapen, fangy, rough, corky or corkscrewed, or that have cracked shoulders, or that feel spongy to the touch or are of poor colour.

Advice to judges   Look for long, uniform, well-shaped roots with good, clean, firm, damage-free skins with a single taproot and foliage trimmed to approximately 75mm.

Condition	5 points
Uniformity	4 points
Shape	4 points
Size	4 points
Colour	3 points
TOTAL	20 points

Broccoli and cauliflowers, coloured headed

Merits   Tight, solid, symmetrical heads of good colour, free from blemish, shown with approximately 50mm of stalk.

Defects   Irregular-shaped heads that are beginning to open or are spongy, lacking freshness or of poor colour.

Advice to judges   Look for tight, solid heads of good colour.

Condition	5 points
Uniformity	4 points
Size	3 points
Shape	3 points
Colour	3 points
TOTAL	18 points

Broccoli, sprouting

Merits   Firm, fresh spears with tight heads of good colour for the cultivar. Shown with approximately 75–100mm of stalk.

Defects   Limp, blown, old spears or heads with spongy texture and poor colour.

Advice to judges   *See Merits and Defects, above*

Condition	5 points
Uniformity	4 points
Size	3 points
Colour	3 points
TOTAL	15 points

Brussels sprouts

Merits   Clean, fresh, solid, tightly closed buttons of good colour and free from blemishes.

Defects   Sprouts that are old, loose-leaved, yellowing, excessively peeled, or that show signs of pest damage or disease.

Advice to judges   Look for unblemished, good-sized, solid sprouts of good colour.

Condition	5 points
Uniformity	4 points
Size	3 points
Colour	3 points
TOTAL	15 points

Cabbages, Chinese

Merits   Fresh, firm, solid heads, outside leaves a fresh green colour, free from pest damage, with roots washed.

Defects   Soft, loose heads that lack freshness or are damaged by pests or disease.

Advice to judges   *See Merits and Defects, above*

Condition	5 points
Uniformity	5 points
Colour	5 points
TOTAL	15 points

Cabbages, green, red or Savoy

Merits Shapely, fresh and solid heads with the surrounding leaves free from any damage or disease with the bloom intact and of good colour. Shape according to cultivar with approximately 50mm of stalk.

Defects Heads that are soft, split, lack freshness, or with the surrounding leaves showing damage due to pests or disease.

Advice to judges *See Merits and Defects, above.* Cabbages may be shown without stalks in collection classes only.

Condition	5 points
Uniformity	3 points
Size	3 points
Shape	2 points
Colour	2 points
TOTAL	15 points

Calabrese

Note: Calabrese sideshoots should be exhibited as Broccoli, sprouting

Merits Fresh, solid, tightly-closed heads of good colour.

Defects Heads that lack freshness or that are irregularly shaped, soft, flowering, or of poor colour.

Advice to judges *See Merits and Defects, above*

Condition	5 points
Uniformity	3 points
Size	3 points
Shape	2 points
Colour	2 points
TOTAL	15 points

Capsicums

*See **Peppers, hot (chilli) or sweet**, p95*

Carrots, long pointed

Merits Fresh, firm, long, smooth roots of good shape and colour maintained for the full length of the root. Skins clean and bright with no evidence of side roots. Foliage trimmed to approximately 75mm.

Defects Roots that are coarse, misshapen or split, have coloured crowns, are fangy, dull, pale, poorly coloured, or that show evidence of pests, disease or of going to seed.

Advice to judges *See Merits and Defects, above*

Condition	5 points
Uniformity	4 points

Size	4 points
Shape	3 points
Colour	4 points
TOTAL	20 points

Carrots, stump rooted

Merits   Fresh roots of good colour and shape with a decided stump. Skin clear and bright. Foliage trimmed to approximately 75mm.

Defects   Roots that are coarse, misshapen or with coloured crowns; are fangy, dull, pale or poorly coloured; showing evidence of pest or disease damage, ribbing, going to seed or lacking a decided stump.

Advice to judges   *See Merits and Defects, above*

Condition	5 points
Uniformity	4 points
Size	3 points
Shape	3 points
Colour	3 points
TOTAL	18 points

Cauliflowers, coloured headed

*See **Broccoli and cauliflowers, coloured headed**, pp78–79*

Cauliflowers, white

Merits   Heads with symmetrical, close, solid, white curd, free from blemish or stain, with approximately 50mm of stalk and foliage neatly trimmed. The curd should form a circle when viewed from above and have a medium-shaped dome when viewed from the side.

Defects   Heads that are spongy, lumpy, becoming loose on the outside edge, not uniformly white, showing signs of pest damage, or that are undeveloped or blown, flat or not symmetrical or showing leaf bracts in the curd.

Advice to judges   *See Merits and Defects above*. Cauliflowers may be shown without stalks in collection classes only.

Condition	5 points
Uniformity	4 points
Size	4 points
Shape	4 points
Colour	3 points
TOTAL	20 points

Celeriac

Merits   Smooth, blemish-free, globe-shaped roots.
Defects   Roots that are rough, split or flat.
Advice to judges   *See Merits and Defects, above*

Condition	5 points
Uniformity	4 points
Size	3 points
Shape	3 points
TOTAL	15 points

Celery, blanched or trench

Merits   Large, well-blanched, firm, clean and crisp stems, free from blemish, pest damage or disease.
Defects   Heads that are small, poorly blanched or showing evidence of pest damage. Stems that are thin, twisted, pithy, split, poorly blanched or showing sideshoots. Hearts that show evidence of rot or that are running to seed.
Advice to judges   Remove all ties. Check the foliage for pest damage. Examine the celery through 360 degrees noting blanch and arrangement of the stems. Look inside to the heart and check for heart rot, seeding, blistering and sideshoots in the stems. Finally, check that the root plate is not split and that the whole exhibit is clean, well-blanched and crisp.

Condition	5 points
Uniformity	4 points
Size	4 points
Shape	4 points
Colour	3 points
TOTAL	20 points

Celery, self-blanching or green

Merits   Fresh, firm, crisp, with clean and blemish-free stalks and leaves. Self-blanching cultivars should be well blanched.
Defects   Small, loose, thin, soft, pithy, or twisted stems, or with heart rot or visible flower stalks.
Advice to judges   *See Celery, blanched or trench, above*

Condition	5 points
Uniformity	4 points
Size	3 points
Shape	3 points
Colour	3 points
TOTAL	18 points

Chards
See Spinach, spinach beet or chards, p100

Chicory, chicons or other types
Merits   Large, solid, crisp, tender, well-formed and well-blanched heads.
Defects   Chicons that are poorly developed, limp or blemished. Heads that are open, soft, loose, limp, tough or badly blanched.
Advice to judges   *See Merits and Defects, above*

Condition	5 points
Uniformity	3 points
Size	2 points
Shape	2 points
Colour	3 points
TOTAL	15 points

Chives
See Salading vegetables, miscellaneous, p98

Corn salad or lambs' lettuce
See Salading vegetables, miscellaneous, p98

Courgettes
Merits   Young, tender fruits of good uniform shape and colour, approximately 150mm in length and approximately 35mm in diameter. Round cultivars should be approximately 75mm in diameter. Of any colour but well matched.
Defects   Fruits that are not young or tender, or that are misshapen, ill-matched or showing evidence of pest damage or disease.
Advice to judges   Specimens may be shown with or without flowers attached.

Condition	4 points
Uniformity	3 points
Size	2 points
Shape	3 points
TOTAL	12 points

Cress
See Salading vegetables, miscellaneous, p98

Cress, American or land
See Salading vegetables, miscellaneous, p98

Cucumbers, grown under protection
Merits   Fresh, young, green, tender, blemish-free, straight fruits of uniform thickness with short handles.
Defects   Fruits that are old, yellowing, crooked, soft, of irregular thickness, showing evidence of pest damage, or are marked by the rubbing or contact with the stalks or leaves, or with long handles.
Advice to judges   Specimens may be shown with or without flowers attached.

Condition	5 points
Uniformity	4 points
Size	3 points
Shape	3 points
Colour	3 points
TOTAL	18 points

Cucumbers, outdoor grown
*For Merits, Defects and Advice to judges, see **Cucumbers, grown under protection**, above*

Condition	5 points
Uniformity	3 points
Size	2 points
Shape	2 points
Colour	3 points
TOTAL	15 points

Dandelion, blanched
See Salading vegetables, miscellaneous, p98

Endive
Merits   Well-formed, well-blanched, crisp, tender heads, free from blemishes.
Defects   Heads that are poorly developed, imperfectly blanched, limp, blemished or that show evidence of pest or disease damage.

Advice to judges   *See Merits and Defects above*

Condition	5 points
Uniformity	4 points
Size	3 points
Colour	3 points
TOTAL	15 points

Fennel
*See **Herbs**, pp86–87*

Fennel, Florence
Merits   Large, clean bulbs with fleshy, swollen leaf bases, free from coarseness or visible flower stems. Foliage trimmed back to approximately 75–100mm but with terminal foliage retained.
Defects   Leaves that are small at the base, coarse or loose. Bulbs that are flat or elongated. Evidence of pest or disease damage.
Advice to judges   *See Merits and Defects, above*

Condition	5 points
Uniformity	3 points
Size	2 points
Shape	2 points
Colour	3 points
TOTAL	15 points

Fruiting vegetables, miscellaneous
(*ie* **other than those dealt with separately**)
Merits   Fresh, young, shapely fruits of good uniform shape and colour that are free from pest or disease damage.
Defects   Fruits that are not fresh and young, that are misshapen, of poor colour, or that show evidence of pest or disease damage.
Advice to judges   Look for ripe, firm, blemish-free, well-coloured fruits of a size according to cultivar with fresh calyces if appropriate.

Condition	4 points
Uniformity	3 points
Colour	2 points
Size	3 points
TOTAL	12 points

Garlic

Merits Well-shaped, solid, clean, well-ripened bulbs with thin necks, with dried stem of approximately 25mm.

Defects Bulbs that are misshapen, soft, poorly ripened or that have thick necks or broken skins.

Advice to judges When displayed for exhibition roots should be removed and bulbs must not be divided into segments (cloves).

Condition	5 points
Uniformity	3 points
Size	2 points
Shape	3 points
Colour	2 points
TOTAL	15 points

Gourds, edible

See Squash, winter, p101

Gourds, ornamental

See Judging Flowers and Ornamental Plants, p130

Herbs

See Glossary definition on p158

Merits Fresh, healthy, clean, blemish-free foliage.

Defects Material that is not fresh and clean, is yellowing or showing other signs of age or pest damage, or has any disease.

Advice to judges *See Merits and Defects, above*

Condition	6 points
Colour	2 points
Size	2 points
TOTAL	10 points

Herbs, growing in pots

See Glossary definition on p158

Merits A sturdy, shapely plant, well furnished with clean, unblemished, healthy foliage. Size of the plant to be proportionate to the size of the pot.

Defects A drawn, undernourished plant with unhealthy, deformed, damaged or diseased foliage.

Advice to judges The presence of healthy flowers on a plant should not be considered a defect, but the decorative value of the flowers should be disregarded.

Condition	6 points
Colour	2 points
Size	2 points
TOTAL	10 points

Kale, curly (borecole)

Merits Fresh, well-developed, blemish-free leaves of good colour and size.

Defects Leaves that are limp, poorly developed, pest damaged or of poor colour.

Advice to judges Look for fresh clean specimens with a well-developed curled leaf pattern.

Condition	5 points
Uniformity	3 points
Size	2 points
Colour	2 points
TOTAL	12 points

Kohlrabi

Merits Fresh, tender, round "bulbs" retaining natural bloom and with small leaf bases; free from damage. Side foliage to be trimmed to approximately 50mm but with terminal foliage retained.

Defects Bulbs that are old, misshapen, lacking natural bloom, that have coarse leaf bases, or that are cracked or damaged.

Advice to judges *See Merits and Defects, above*

Condition	5 points
Uniformity	3 points
Size	2 points
Shape	2 points
TOTAL	12 points

Leaf vegetables, miscellaneous
(*ie* other than those dealt with separately)

Merits Fresh, healthy, clean, blemish-free foliage.

Defects Material that is not fresh and clean, is yellowing or showing other signs of age or pest damage, or has any disease.

Advice to judges Look for large, well-formed leaves of good colour, free from damage and disease.

Condition	6 points
Colour	2 points
Size	2 points
TOTAL	10 points

Leeks, blanched or intermediate
(see note on pp38–39 and Glossary, p160)

Merits   Clean, firm, solid, parallel-sided, long barrels with no sign of softness or splits, with a tight button and free from bulbing and ribbiness. Foliage that is turgid and free from pest and disease damage.

Defects   Leeks that are soft, thin, tapering, short-shafted, imperfectly blanched, discoloured or bulbous, or that have diseased or damaged leaves.

Advice to judges   Specimens must be over 150mm from root plate to button. Foliage should be dark green in colour, turgid, with no rust, pest damage or evidence of seeding. Barrels should be firm and sound with no sign of tapering or bulbing. Roots should be fresh with a sound root plate intact. Good specimens will have a long, distinct blanch that is in proportion to the circumference of the barrel. In close competition measuring the length and girth of each exhibit will aid selection.

Blanched leeks are over 350mm in length; Intermediate leeks are between 150mm and 350mm in length. In small, local shows judges may consider leeks over 150mm in length as blanched leeks.

Condition	6 points
Uniformity	4 points
Size	4 points
Shape	3 points
Colour	3 points
TOTAL	20 points

Leeks (pot)
(see note on pp38–39 and Glossary, p160)

Merits   Firm, solid heavy leeks with unbroken, clean and unblemished skins. Fresh foliage that is free from damage, pests or disease. Barrels that are parallel and well blanched with sound root plate and roots intact. Blanch must not be greater than 150mm from the root plate to the button.

Defects   Leeks that are soft, thin, small, with a split button, shaft too long or ribby, evidence of seedhead. Barrels that taper or that are bulbous. Malformation or damage of any part including the root plate.

Advice to judges   First check the length of the barrels. Specimens over 150mm in length will be automatically disqualified. Foliage should be fresh, green, firm, damage and disease free and with no evidence of seeding. Barrels should be straight and well-blanched with a sound root plate and fresh roots.

Condition	6 points
Uniformity	4 points
Size	4 points
Shape	3 points
Colour	3 points
TOTAL	20 points

• **Note:** The National Pot Leek Society give additional points for volume or cubic capacity measured on volume of blanched shaft to tight 150mm (6in) button (*ie* from basal plate to lowest unbroken leaf, including the veil where present and around the barrel). One point for every 164cm^3 (10in^3) and decimal point for part of 164cm^3 (10in^3.) Tables for the calculation of cubic capacity are obtainable from the Secretary of the National Pot Leek Society.

Lettuces, butterhead, cos or crisp
(see note on p39)
Merits Fresh, tender, unbroken, blemish-free heads of appropriate colour.
Defects Heads that are limp, show signs of bolting, are blemished or are of poor colour.
Advice to judges Downpoint specimens that have soft or broken-leaved heads, are old, of a poor colour, or that show pest or disease damage.

Condition	5 points
Uniformity	4 points
Firmness and texture	3 points
Colour	3 points
TOTAL	15 points

Lettuces, loose-leaf
(see note on p39)
Merits Fresh, clean, tender, unbroken, blemish-free heads of appropriate colour.
Defects Heads that are limp, not clean, that show signs of bolting, are blemished or are of poor colour.
Advice to judges Downpoint specimens that have soft or broken-leaved heads, are old, of a poor colour, or that show pest or disease damage or soil splash.

Condition	5 points
Uniformity	4 points
Colour	3 points
TOTAL	12 points

Marjoram
See **Herbs**, *pp86–87*

Marrows
Merits   Fresh, young, tender fruits that should be less than 350mm in length or, in the case of round cultivars, approximately 500mm in circumference.
Defects   Fruits that are not young or tender or that are blemished, misshapen or ill-matched. Old and overripe marrows or fruits that exceed 350mm in length, or in the case of round-fruited cultivars, 500mm in circumference.
Advice to judges   Downpoint specimens that are old, hard, or that are larger than the recommended sizes, or that are lacking uniformity.

Condition, including tenderness	6 points
Uniformity	4 points
Size	3 points
Shape	2 points
TOTAL	15 points

Mint
See **Herbs**, *pp86–87*

Mushrooms
Stage of development should be stated in the Schedule *ie* "Button", "Closed Cap" or "Open Cap".
Merits   Mushrooms that are well formed with unbroken edges and free from blemishes. If the gills are visible they should be pink in colour.
Defects   Mushrooms that are blemished, misshapen, show any signs of shrivelling, are flattened, have broken edges or blackening gills.
Advice to judges   Look for well-formed specimens with unbroken cap edges, free from blemish, with gills of a good colour where appropriate.

Condition and freshness	7 points
Uniformity	4 points
Colour	4 points
TOTAL	15 points

Mustard or rape
See **Salading vegetables, miscellaneous**, *p98*

Okra

Merits Fresh, slender-pointed fruits, free from blemishes and less than 100mm long.

Defects Fruits that are misshapen, shrivelled, dull or poorly coloured, or over 100mm long.

Advice to judges Downpoint fruits that are bulky, misshapen, old or poorly coloured, under- or oversized, or that lack uniformity.

Condition	6 points
Uniformity	5 points
Size	4 points
Colour	3 points
TOTAL	18 points

Onions, large exhibition, over 250g

Merits Large firm, well-ripened bulbs with thin necks and unbroken skins, free from any damage or disease. Sound and intact root plates.

Defects Bulbs that are small, misshapen, lopsided or blemished, or that have soft or thick necks, or indicate moisture present under the skin, or have broken outer skins or have unsound root plates.

Advice to judges All specimens must be weighed and any of 250g or under must be disqualified. Look for large, uniform, well-ripened bulbs, of good shape, free from any blemish, with roots trimmed and necks neatly tied with uncoloured raffia. At early summer shows bulbs may be shown with tops trimmed, bulbs either dressed or as grown with roots washed.

Condition	6 points
Uniformity	4 points
Size	5 points
Shape	3 points
Colour	2 points
TOTAL	20 points

Onions, 250g or under

Merits Firm, thin-necked, blemish-free bulbs grown from either seed or sets with well-ripened, unbroken skins free from any damage or disease.

Defects Bulbs that are too small or in excess of 250g, thick-necked, misshapen, blemished, or that have broken skins or have been skinned excessively.

Advice to judges All specimens must be weighed and any over 250g must be disqualified. Bulbs should be as near to

250g as possible, of good form and alike in size, shape and colour.

Condition	5 points
Uniformity	3 points
Size	2 points
Shape	3 points
Colour	2 points
TOTAL	15 points

• **Note:** If a class for onions grown from sets is required, the same judging attributes and pointing should be used as for Onions, 250g or under, but with no weight restriction.

Onions, green salad

Merits Fresh, tender, young, non-bulbous plants having white bases with clean roots attached.

Defects Plants that have leaves that are damaged, yellow-tipped or have been trimmed; or plants that are bulbous or have bases other than white.

Advice to judges Look for plants showing good uniformity that are free of pest and disease damage.

Condition	3 points
Uniformity	3 points
Size	2 points
Shape	2 points
Colour	2 points
TOTAL	12 points

Onions on ropes

Onions on ropes are not eligible for collection classes.

Merits Firm, thin-necked blemish-free bulbs grown from either seed or sets with well-ripened, unbroken skins free from any damage or disease. Rope neatly tied and presented.

Defects Bulbs that are too small, thick-necked, misshapen, blemished, or that have broken skins or have been skinned excessively. Rope untidy or not well presented.

Advice to judges Bulbs should be of good form and alike in size, shape and colour.

Condition	5 points
Uniformity	3 points
Size	2 points
Shape	3 points
Colour	2 points
Presentation	5 points
TOTAL	20 points

Onions, pickling

Merits Small, firm, well-ripened uniform bulbs, approximately 30mm in diameter.

Defects Bulbs that are soft, unripe, non-uniform, or that are too large or too small, or a poor shape or colour, or have broken skins.

Advice to judges Look for well-formed bulbs of the appropriate size that are firm, uniform and free from any blemish.

Condition	3 points
Uniformity	3 points
Size	2 points
Shape	2 points
Colour	2 points
TOTAL	12 points

Oriental brassicas, flowering stalk types
eg **choi-sum**
See Broccoli, sprouting, p79

Oriental brassicas, heading types
eg **pak-choi types**

Merits Fresh, tender, firm, well-developed uniform heads, free from pest damage or disease.

Defects Poorly formed heads showing pest damage or disease.

Advice to judges Look for clean, fresh, tender, blemish-free heads.

Condition	5 points
Uniformity	5 points
Colour	5 points
TOTAL	15 points

Oriental brassicas, loose-leaf or rosette types *eg* **leaf mustards, mibuna, mizuna**

Merits Fresh, tender, unbroken, well-developed plants, free from pest damage or disease.

Defects Heads that are limp or show signs of bolting, are blemished or show poor colour.

Advice to judges Look for fresh, well-developed plants that are free from any blemish or disease.

Condition	5 points
Uniformity	4 points
Colour	3 points
TOTAL	12 points

Parsley
See Herbs, pp86–87

Parsnips
Merits Long, large, well-developed, well-shouldered, shapely, white roots, smooth skinned and free from side roots or blemishes and with taproot intact. Foliage trimmed to approximately 75mm.

Defects Roots that lack size or good, clean shoulders, that are misshapen or have rough, discoloured skins, side roots, blemishes or canker.

Advice to judges Check that shoulders are symmetrical and free from any blemish. Roots should be fresh and firm with no blemish or disease, alike in size shape and colour. Good weight is considered more important than length.

Condition	5 points
Uniformity	4 points
Size	4 points
Shape	4 points
Colour	3 points
TOTAL	20 points

Peas
Merits Large, long fresh, smooth pods of good colour with bloom intact and with stalks, free from disease or pest damage and well filled with tender peas.

Defects Pods that are small, not fresh or of poor colour or having very imperfect bloom, or that have no stalks, or that are diseased or pest damaged or poorly filled or containing peas that are old or maggoty.

Advice to judges Look for large, fresh pods, uniform in size, of good colour with bloom intact, pest and disease free. Open a pod from each exhibit and observe the contents, which should be well filled with blemish-free peas. Where necessary, hold pods up to the light to check for good pod set.

Condition	6 points
Uniformity	4 points
Size	4 points
Fullness of pod	4 points
Colour	2 points
TOTAL	20 points

Peas, mangetout or snap

Merits Fresh pods of good colour with bloom intact, free from disease and pest damage. Peas should not be overdeveloped.

Defects Pods that are not fresh or of poor colour, or having imperfect bloom, or that are diseased, pest damaged, or containing seeds that are poorly set or that are old or maggoty.

Advice to judges For mangetout the pods should be flat with seeds present but undeveloped. For snap peas, pods should be fleshy and snap easily. Where necessary, hold pods up to the light to check for good pod set.

Condition	5 points
Uniformity	4 points
Size	4 points
Colour	2 points
TOTAL	15 points

Peppers, hot (chilli) or sweet

Merits Fresh, bright fruits with clear skins of a colour according to cultivar.

Defects Fruits that are dull, misshapen, shrivelled or poorly coloured.

Advice to judges Look for uniform, fresh, bright fruits.

Condition	5 points
Uniformity	3 points
Size	2 points
Shape	2 points
Colour	3 points
TOTAL	15 points

Potatoes

Merits Medium-sized tubers of approximately 175–225g each; shapely, clean, clear-skinned; eyes few and shallow.

Defects Tubers that are very small or very large, damaged or misshapen, with speckled or patchy skins, that are greening or have excessively deep eyes.

Advice to judges Look for clean, blemish free, medium-sized uniform tubers, well-shaped with shallow eyes.

Condition	5 points
Uniformity	5 points
Size	3 points
Shape	4 points
Eyes	3 points
TOTAL	20 points

Pumpkins

Merits A shapely, firm fruit of good colour and ripeness, with stalk attached.

Defects A fruit that is misshapen, soft, unevenly ripened or with a blemished or marked skin, or lacking its stalk.

Advice to judges Look for well-formed, large, shapely fruit that are firm, of good colour and ripeness with stalk attached.

Condition	4 points
Size	3 points
Colour	3 points
TOTAL	10 points

Radishes, Oriental or winter

Merits Fresh roots, well coloured and free from blemishes.

Defects Roots tough, spongy, of a dull colour or blemished.

Advice to judges Look for roots that are young, tender, uniform and blemish-free.

Condition	5 points
Uniformity	4 points
Size	3 points
Colour	3 points
TOTAL	15 points

Radishes, small salad

Merits Fresh, firm, young, tender, well-coloured roots, free from blemishes. Foliage that is free of pest and disease damage. Foliage trimmed to approximately 40mm.

Defects Roots that are old, tough, misshapen, limp or that show pest or disease damage or evidence of running to seed.

Advice to judges Look for roots that are young, tender, uniform and blemish-free.

Condition	3 points
Uniformity	3 points
Size	2 points
Colour	2 points
TOTAL	10 points

Rhubarb, forced

Merits Fresh, firm, straight, long, brightly coloured stalks with well developed colouring and small, undeveloped leaves.

Defects Stalks that are limp, crooked, small, thin or dull-coloured, or have developed leaf blades or that have had leaves removed.

Advice to judges Look for fresh, firm, straight stalks of uniform overall length and weight with good colour.

Condition	4 points
Uniformity	3 points
Size	3 points
Shape	2 points
Colour	3 points
TOTAL	15 points

Rhubarb, natural

Merits Fresh, straight, long, tender stalks with well-developed colouring with leaf blades trimmed back to approximately 75mm.

Defects Stalks that are small, limp, crooked, stunted, tough, damaged, or lacking in red colouring.

Advice to judges Look for fresh, straight stalks of uniform overall length and weight with good colour. It is advisable to break a stalk in each exhibit to test for freshness and colour.

Condition	3 points
Uniformity	3 points
Shape	3 points
Colour	3 points
TOTAL	12 points

Root vegetables, miscellaneous
(*ie* other than those dealt with separately)

Merits Clear-skinned, solid, shapely roots that are free of pest and disease damage.

Defects Roots that are very small or very large, have patchy skins, that are spongy, of irregular shape or that are pest or disease damaged.

Advice to judges *See Merits and Defects above*

Condition	5 points
Uniformity	4 points
Size	2 points
Shape	2 points
Colour	2 points
TOTAL	15 points

Sage
*See **Herbs**, pp86–87*

Salading vegetables, miscellaneous
(*ie* **other than those dealt with separately**)
See Glossary, p162

Merits Material that is young, fresh, clean and of attractive appearance.

Defects Material that is not young or is limp, soiled, pest damaged or at all unattractive.

Advice to judges Look for fresh, clean, young, disease free specimens that are uniform in size and colour according to type.

Condition	4 points
Uniformity	2 points
Size	2 points
Colour	2 points
TOTAL	10 points

Salsify and scorzonera

Merits Large, shapely, evenly tapering, clean, smooth-skinned roots, free from side roots. Scorzonera should be dark in colour. Tops trimmed to approximately 75mm.

Defects Roots that are small, misshapen or taper unevenly or are fangy or lack a clean, smooth skin. Scorzonera roots that are pale.

Advice to judges Look for clean, well-tapered roots that are large without being coarse, and free from blemishes or side roots.

Condition	5 points
Uniformity	4 points
Size	2 points
Shape	2 points
Colour	2 points
TOTAL	15 points

Savory, summer or winter
See Herbs, pp86–87

Scorzonera
See Salsify and scorzonera, above

Seakale

Merits Stout, crisp, well-blanched shoots with leaf blades undeveloped.

Defects Shoots that are spindly, limp or poorly blanched or that have developed leaf blades.

Advice to judges   Look for well-balanced, crisp heads of good size and free of leaf development.

Condition	5 points
Uniformity	4 points
Size	2 points
Blanch	2 points
Freedom from leaf-development	2 points
TOTAL	15 points

Shallots, large exhibition

Merits   Large, firm, well-ripened, round, shapely bulbs of good form with thin necks and of good size and colour.
Defects   Bulbs that are asymmetrical or soft or that have thick necks, are poorly ripened or have broken or blemished skins, or bulbs that have been over-skinned.
Advice to judges   Look for large, shapely, round, uniform, disease-free bulbs that are well presented with tops neatly tied with uncoloured raffia. Over-skinning will reveal greening or purpling of the base.

Condition	6 points
Uniformity	3 points
Size	3 points
Shape	3 points
Colour	3 points
TOTAL	18 points

Shallots, pickling

Merits   Round, solid, well-ripened bulbs of good form and colour with thin necks. Bulbs must not exceed 30mm in diameter.
Defects   Bulbs that are asymmetrical or soft or that have thick necks, are poorly ripened, or have split, broken or blemished skins, or bulbs that have been over-skinned.
Advice to judges   Pickling shallots must not exceed 30mm in diameter. Check that each bulb passes through the designated ring easily and unaided. Disqualify exhibits that have oversize bulbs. Ensure that all bulbs are well presented with tops neatly tied with uncoloured raffia. Over-skinning will reveal greening or purpling of the base.

Condition	5 points
Uniformity	4 points
Size	2 points
Shape	2 points
Colour	2 points
TOTAL	15 points

Spinach, spinach beet or chards

Merits Fresh, undamaged, well-formed, uniformly coloured leaves.

Defects Leaves that are limp, broken, of poor colour, damaged or diseased.

Advice to judges Look for fresh, large, well-formed leaves of good colour, free from damage or disease. Chards should have broad, flat leaves with good colour appropriate to the cultivar.

Condition	5 points
Uniformity	3 points
Size	2 points
Colour	2 points
TOTAL	12 points

Spinach, New Zealand

Merits Fresh, dark-green tips without evidence of flowers.

Defects Small, ageing, diseased or yellowing tips or those that show evidence of flowering.

Advice to judges Look for fresh, dark green tips that are approximately 75mm long.

Condition	5 points
Uniformity	2 points
Size	2 points
Colour	3 points
TOTAL	12 points

Squash, summer

(See Glossary, pp162–163)

Merits Young, tender, shapely fruits of any colour but well matched.

Defects Fruits that are not young or tender or that are misshapen, ill-matched or blemished.

Advice to judges Look for young, tender, shapely fruits. Specimens may be shown with or without flowers attached.

Condition	4 points
Uniformity	3 points
Size	2 points
Shape	3 points
TOTAL	12 points

Squash, winter
(See Glossary, pp162–163)
Merits A shapely, large, firm fruit of even colour and ripeness with stalk attached.
Defects A fruit that is misshapen, soft, unevenly ripened or with spotted or marked skin or lacking its stalk.
Advice to judges Look for well-formed, large, shapely fruit that are firm, of good colour and ripeness with stalk attached.

Condition	4 points
Size	3 points
Colour	3 points
TOTAL	10 points

Swedes
See Turnips and swedes, p103

Sweet corn
Merits Fresh, well-formed, cylindrical cobs, well set throughout including the tips, with straight rows of undamaged, plump, tender grains and with fresh green husks.
Defects Cobs that are not fresh or that are unduly tapered or have irregular rows of grain or are badly set or that have husks that are shrivelled and straw coloured, or have anthers between them.
Advice to judges Cobs should be fresh, of good size, well-formed, with green husks and silks attached. Pull down the husks to reveal the grains, which should be fresh, plump and not shrivelled. Well-grown cobs should be well set to the tip.

Condition	5 points
Uniformity	4 points
Size	3 points
Set of grain	3 points
Colour	3 points
TOTAL	18 points

Tarragon
See Herbs, pp86–87

Thyme
See Herbs, pp86–87

Tomatoes, large (*eg* beefsteak type)

Merits   Large fruits not less than 75mm in diameter. Shapely, ripe but firm and, well-coloured with fresh calyces attached.

Defects   Small, misshapen, unripe or overripe, or of a dull colour, green-backed, pest or disease damaged or lacking calyces.

Advice to judges   Look for large, fresh, firm, well-shaped, uniform fruits of good colour, not polished and with fresh calyces.

Condition	5 points
Uniformity	3 points
Size	3 points
Shape	2 points
Colour	2 points
TOTAL	15 points

Tomatoes, medium

Merits   Well-shaped, clear-skinned, rounded fruits (approximately 60mm in diameter) ripe but firm. Richly coloured fruits with fresh calyces attached.

Defects   Fruits that are small or very large, of uneven shape, unripe or overripe, of a dull colour or green-backed, blemished, or that lack calyces.

Advice to judges   Look for firm, uniform fruits, free from blemishes, ripe yet firm, with fresh calyces and natural bloom.

Condition	5 points
Uniformity	4 points
Size	3 points
Shape	3 points
Colour	3 points
TOTAL	18 points

Tomatoes, plum

*See **Tomatoes, medium**, above (except that they should not be rounded)*

Tomatoes, small-fruited, cherry or small plum cultivars

Merits Fresh, ripe but firm, well-coloured fruits, blemish-free, and with fresh calyces attached. Size should not exceed 35mm in diameter.

Defects Fruits that are oversize or inappropriately small for the cultivar, or unevenly shaped; unripe or overripe, green-backed or without calyces attached.

Advice to judges Look for ripe, firm, blemish-free, well-coloured fruits of the appropriate size, not polished and with fresh calyces.

Condition	3 points
Uniformity	3 points
Size	2 points
Shape	2 points
Colour	2 points
TOTAL	12 points

Turnips and swedes

Merits Clear-skinned, solid, shapely roots with small taproots and no side roots, pest and disease free. Turnips: size and shape according to cultivar. Swedes: medium-sized.

Defects Roots that are very small or very large, have patchy skins, that are spongy, of irregular shape or that have large taproots or side roots.

Advice to judges Look for well-grown, clean specimens, uniform in size, shape and colour, pest and disease free with no evidence of multiple tap roots.

Condition	5 points
Uniformity	4 points
Size	2 points
Shape	2 points
Colour	2 points
TOTAL	15 points

Watercress

*See **Salading vegetables, miscellaneous**, p98*

THE JUDGING OF FLOWERS AND ORNAMENTAL PLANTS

Where a scale of points is given in this section it should only apply to that category, and not when different categories are compared.

In assessing the merits of most exhibits of flowers and some exhibits of pot plants consideration should be given to condition and uniformity.

Condition   An exhibit is in good condition when the material of which it consists is in the most perfect stage of its possible beauty and is fresh and free from damage due to weather, pests, diseases, faulty handling or any other cause.

Uniformity   An exhibit is uniform when items of which it consists are alike in age, size and form.

 The way in which an exhibit of flowers or ornamental plants is staged is particularly important. But in the following scales no points are allocated to "arrangement" because, although attractive presentation will automatically influence the judges, the extent to which it should and will do so depends not so much on the kind of flower or plant as on the nature of the exhibit for which the schedule calls, *eg* a single bloom or a vase of many blooms. In all cases, however, an exhibit that is arranged in such a way as to display the merits of the flowers or plants to best advantage will inevitably and rightly make a more favourable impression on the judges, even though the flowers or plants in the two exhibits may be of equal merit.

Annual, biennial, bulbous and herbaceous plants in flower
(other than those for which separate criteria are given elsewhere in this section)

Vases of one kind
Merits   Good fresh condition. A good proportion of flowers fully developed and appropriately positioned on their stem(s). The petals should be properly positioned on the flowers and of a shape, texture and colour typical of the species or cultivar. The foliage should be clean, healthy and undamaged by weather or pests. Stems should be typical of the species or

cultivar, and in the case of flowers that bloom in spikes such as larkspurs and hyacinths or in crowns, such as hippeastrums and crown imperials, should be straight and firm right to the tip with the flowers evenly spaced and the open florets touching or almost touching one another.

Defects Poor condition. Some flowers either undeveloped or past their peak. Petals unnaturally twisted or misshapen or of poor texture or colour for the species or cultivar. Foliage or flowers that are mud-splashed, or showing signs of insect or fungal damage. Stems that are untypically short, twisted, weak or bent.

Advice to judges For show purposes, the ornamental bracts surrounding the flowers of plants such as *Euphorbia*, *Salvia sclarea* (clary) and *Salvia horminum* are considered to be a part of the flower and the plant may be judged as "in bloom" if these are fully expanded even though the true flowers are not completely open.

Condition of flowers and stems	6 points
Uniformity	4 points
Shape and texture of flowers and foliage	6 points
Colour	4 points
TOTAL	20 points

Mixed vases

The above criteria may be applied equally as well to vases of mixed flowers from different genera, species or cultivars, *ie* not less than three different plants, but the judging criteria should be adjusted as follows. The inclusion of foliage from plants other than those of the flowers/seedheads/fruits being exhibited in the mixed vase is not encouraged.

Condition and quality of flowers, foliage and stems	8 points
Colour, texture and arrangement	6 points
Symmetry and balance of exhibit (presentation)	6 points
TOTAL	20 points

Ornamental trees and shrubs in flower or fruit (including seedheads)

(other than those for which separate criteria are given elsewhere in this section)

Vases of one kind

Merits   Good fresh condition. A good proportion of flowers or fruits fully developed and well positioned on shapely, well-balanced sprays, stems or branches. Individual flowers or fruits well shaped and of a texture, size and colour typical of the species or cultivar. Fresh, healthy, clean, undamaged foliage of good colour and of a size and pattern typical of the species or cultivar.

Defects   Poor, limp or starved condition. Flowers or fruits that are misshapen, undeveloped or past their best or sparsely distributed. Sprays, stems or branches that are unevenly developed, unnaturally twisted or stunted or not typical of the species or cultivar. Foliage that shows signs of damage by insects, weather or disease or is under or over-sized for the species or cultivar.

Advice to judges   For show purposes, the ornamental bracts surrounding the flowers of plants such as *Cornus kousa*, *Davidia* and *Euphorbia* are considered to be a part of the flower and the plant may be judged as "in bloom" if these are fully expanded even though the true flowers are not completely open.

Condition of flowers/fruit and foliage	5 points
Shape and texture of flowers, fruit and foliage	5 points
Colour	4 points
Stems/sprays/branches	3 points
Balance or symmetry of the exhibit	3 points
TOTAL	20 points

Mixed vases

The above criteria maybe applied equally as well to vases of mixed sprays from different genera, species or cultivars *ie* not less than three different plants, but the judging criteria should be adjusted as follows. The inclusion of foliage from plants other than those of the flowers/seedheads/fruits being exhibited in the mixed vase is not encouraged.

Condition and quality	8 points
Colour, texture and arrangement	6 points
Symmetry and balance of exhibit (presentation)	6 points
TOTAL	20 points

Alpine-house and rock-garden plants

Merits A plant of a size suitable for an alpine house or rock garden and hardy enough to survive an average winter in a frost-free house. (It need not be a native of mountainous regions and may be a perennial herbaceous plant, an annual or a shrub.) Other things being equal, preference should be given to a plant that is difficult to grow. A plant "in character" (*ie* its character in nature). Many perfect open blooms in a plant grown for its flower. Closeness and firmness in a cushion plant. Rarity (*ie* in cultivation). A conifer or a shrub on its own roots should be preferred to a grafted specimen with the exception of certain genera, such as *Pinus*, that are usually propagated by grafting. Colourful foliage in a plant grown for the colour of its leaves.

Defects A plant that attains too great a size to be suitable for an alpine house or rock garden or that is not hardy enough to survive an average winter in an unheated house. A plant that is common in cultivation or easy to grow if in competition with one that is rare in cultivation or difficult to grow. A plant that does not conform to its character in nature. A plant that is grown for its flowers but has few flowers or flowers that are not open or are past their best. A cushion plant that is loose or patchy. A conifer or shrub that has been grafted, with the exception of certain genera, such as *Pinus*, that are usually propagated by grafting, or that has been clipped or artificially dwarfed. A plant grown for its coloured foliage but lacking colour.

Suitability	2 points
Rarity in cultivation	2 points
In character	2 points
Cultivation	4 points
TOTAL	10 points

Auriculas, alpine, double and show

Merits   Well-balanced, healthy foliage. A strong stem, sufficiently long to bear the truss well above the foliage, arising from a single rosette. A truss carried on pedicels sufficiently long to avoid overlapping of the pips. A circular tube, filled by the anthers, hiding the stigma.

• **Alpine auriculas:** A golden, yellow cream or white centre, without farina (a mealy coating). A richly coloured but not necessarily dark edge, shaded to a paler tint.

• **Double auriculas:** The pips should be of rich or clear colours. Doubling to be symmetrical and to fill the corolla effectively. All pips should possess the same degree of doubling.

• **Show auriculas:** A truss consisting of not fewer than five fully developed pips (three in a seedling). A perfectly flat, round, smooth-edged pip consisting of lobes without notches or serrations. Tube of a deep yellow colour. A pure white, smooth paste (inner circular zone of the petals, surrounding the central tube), free from crack or blemish, circular in outline. A dense ground-colour, forming a perfect circle near the paste, the darker and richer the colour the better, though red should not be regarded as a fault. A bright green, grey or white edge of about the same width as the ground-colour. In "selfs" the colour should be uniform throughout and without shading. The paste should be as required in the edged section and should be about equal in width to that of the border colour.

Defects   Foliage that is ill-balanced, limp or unhealthy. A stem that is weak or short, allowing the pips to overlap. A tube that is irregular or has a visible stigma.

• **Alpine auriculas:** An edge that is not richly coloured.

• **Double auriculas:** Pips that are not of rich or clear colours. Doubling that is asymmetrical or lacking effect or shows a marked decrease from the earliest to the latest pip.

• **Show auriculas:** A truss that has fewer than five well-developed pips (three in a seedling). A pip that is not flat, circular or smooth-edged or has fewer than six lobes or has notched or serrated lobes. A tube that is pale-coloured. A paste that is not pure white or is rough, cracked or blemished or lacks a circular outline. A ground-colour that does not have a perfectly circular outline or that lacks density or richness. An edge that is not self-coloured or that is wider than half the width of the paste.

Scales of points

Alpine auriculas
Foliage, stem and pedicels	8 points
Pips	4 points
Tube	2 points
Centre	3 points
Edge	3 points
TOTAL	20 points

Double auriculas
Foliage, stem and pedicels	7 points
Colour of pips	4 points
Doubling – symmetry and effect	6 points
Doubling – degree	3 points
TOTAL	20 points

Show auriculas other than "selfs"
Foliage, stem and pedicels	7 points
Pips	2 points
Tube	2 points
Paste	3 points
Ground-colour	3 points
Edge	3 points
TOTAL	20 points

"selfs"
Foliage, stem and pedicels	7 points
Pips	2 points
Tube	3 points
Paste	4 points
Border	4 points
TOTAL	20 points

Begonias, double tuberous

Merits A well-balanced plant, bearing flowers in size and number proportionate to the size of the plant and to the cultivar. Large flowers of good substance, circular in outline with broad overlapping petals culminating in one centre. Colour decided and clear. In picotee cultivars the colours should not run one into another. Foliage and flowers that are clean, healthy and undamaged. Stems that are stout and erect.

Defects An ill-balanced plant, carrying flowers that are few or small for the size of the plant or the cultivar where known. Small flowers, of poor texture or irregular outline or having divided centres. Long, narrow petals. Pale, damaged or spotted foliage or flowers. Spindly, weak stems.

Advice to judges   It is not necessary for the plant to be shown for all-round effect. Supports for the blooms are permitted.

Plant	5 points
Stems	3 points
Form of flower	6 points
Colour	3 points
Foliage	3 points
TOTAL	20 points

Bonsai

A bonsai is essentially a tree encouraged to conform in all respects with an ordinary tree, except for its miniature size. Natural dwarf trees are not bonsai, unless trained to look like a large natural tree in shape and restricted to a size smaller than their own maximum potential. A bonsai and its container must together present a satisfactory, well-balanced and aesthetic unity.

Merits   A strong, well-shaped trunk tapering upwards, merging naturally with the growing medium. Surface roots fanning out from the base of the trunk and gradually disappearing into the soil. Well-proportioned head of branches well-spaced and set on the trunk and without scars or marks of training. A tree looking as natural as possible with all its parts in proportion. Pots, preferably in monochrome glaze, in proportion to the tree. Polychrome pots are permissible but are best used for non-flowering and non-fruiting specimens. Tree so placed in the pot as to create a visual balance. Flowers, fruit and foliage in proportion to the size of tree. Trees planted well raised in the pot, so that the bole can be seen clearly over the rim of the pot when viewed at eye level.

Defects   Weak, badly shaped trunks or those that look like sticks or branches stuck in the ground. Badly spaced, cut, scarred or crossed branches. Noticeable artificial training; uncharacteristic growth for species. Snagged or abruptly cut roots visible above the soil or dead fibrous roots standing in the air. Trees out of balance. Flowers, fruit or foliage out of proportion to the size of the tree. Soil surface and bole of trunk sunk well below the rim of the pot. Unnecessary additional ornaments or decoration.

Cacti and succulents

Merits   A large specimen for the particular species, hybrid or cultivar; well-balanced and in good health. It should be free from defects of any sort including damaged or missing spines, distorted bodies or leaves, abnormal marks or lesions (except close to soil level), or defective "bloom". Other things being equal, a plant that shows evidence of flowering will be preferred to one that does not. A species, hybrid or cultivar that is difficult to cultivate will be preferred to one that is easy.

Defects   A specimen that is small for the particular species, hybrid or cultivar, is in poor health or shows evidence of pest infestation at any time in its life. A specimen that has damaged or missing spines, distortion of bodies or leaves, scarring of body or leaves, defective "bloom" or that is poorly presented. A specimen of flowering size that shows no evidence of flowering, if in competition with one that does.

Condition	6 points
Maturity (age in cultivation)	5 points
Freedom from pests and diseases	2 points
Difficulty of cultivation	3 points
Rarity in cultivation	1 point
Presentation	3 points
TOTAL	20 points

Carnations, border (including picotees)

Border carnations may be classed according to colour as follows:

Selfs, which must be of one clear colour.

Fancies, which must have a clear ground-colour and be marked or suffused by a contrasting colour or colours.

Picotees, which must have a clear ground-colour, with an even, unbroken margin of contrasting colour around every petal.

Fancies and *picotees* may be further divided according to their ground-colour. Cloves may be any colour or colours, but must possess a strong clove scent.

Merits   Good condition. Flowers that are fresh, symmetrical and circular in outline, with no hole or gap in the centre. Firm petals with smooth edges, slight indentation permitted. Guard-petals that are large, broad, smooth and carried at right angles to the calyx. Inner petals that lie regularly and smoothly over the guard-petals, though the centre petals may stand up somewhat and form a crown. Calyx should be unbroken. Strong stems. Colour or colours clear, bright and well defined. A strong scent. Uniformity.

Defects   Unsatisfactory condition. Holes or gaps should not appear in the centre of the flower. Flowers that are small or not circular in outline. Petals that lack substance or have serrated edges or show a marked tendency to incurve or are so numerous as to appear crowded. Guard-petals that are small, narrow or are incurved or recurved. Split calyces and stems that are weak or lacking uniformity. Unless specifically permitted by the schedule, exhibits with stem supports or calyx bands must be disqualified.

Condition	7 points
Form (of flower)	7 points
Colour	3 points
Size	3 points
TOTAL	20 points

Carnations, perpetual-flowering

Perpetual-flowering carnations may be classed according to colour as follows:

Selfs, which must be of one clear colour.

Fancies, which must have a clear ground-colour and be marked or suffused with a contrasting colour or colours. Fancies may be further divided according to their ground-colour.

Merits   Good condition. Flowers that are large, symmetrical circular in outline and that have full centres. Guard-petals that are flat, firm and well formed. (The edges may be either smooth or regularly serrated.) Calyx unbroken. Strong stems proportionate in length and thickness to the size of the flowers. Clear and bright colours. A strong scent. Uniformity.

Defects   Unsatisfactory condition. Flowers that are coarse, small or asymmetrical. Split calyces with weak, clumsy or short stems, lacking scent and uniformity. Unless specifically permitted by the schedule, exhibits with stem supports or calyx bands must be disqualified.

Condition	7 points
Form (of flower)	7 points
Colour	3 points
Size	3 points
TOTAL	20 points

Chrysanthemums

For shows organised by the National Chrysanthemum Society (NCS) or for chrysanthemum classes in shows organised by societies affiliated to the NCS, the use of the NCS scale of points may be obligatory. Details of these scales may be obtained from the Secretary of the National Chrysanthemum Society.

The following paragraphs contain advice about judging most of the different sections into which chrysanthemum cultivars have been classified.

Classification

Late-flowering (indoor cultivars)

Section 1	Large Exhibition (Incurving and Reflexing)
Section 2	Medium Exhibition
Section 3	Exhibition Incurved
Section 4	Reflexed Decoratives
Section 5	Intermediate Decoratives
Section 6	Anemones
Section 7	Singles
Section 8	Pompons
Section 9	Sprays
Section 10	Spidery, Plumed and Feathery
Section 11	Any other types

October-flowering

Section 13	Incurved Decoratives
Section 14	Reflexed Decoratives
Section 15	Intermediate Decoratives
Section 16	Large October-flowering
Section 17	Singles, October-flowering
Section 18	Pompons, October-flowering
Section 19	Sprays, October-flowering
Section 20	Any other types, October-flowering

Early-flowering (outdoor cultivars)

Section 23	Incurved Decoratives
Section 24	Reflexed Decoratives
Section 25	Intermediate Decoratives
Section 26	Anemones
Section 27	Singles
Section 28	Pompons
Section 29	Sprays
Section 30	Any other types

Cultivars in Sections 13 to 20 (October-flowering types) may normally be shown in classes at shows for early-flowering

types but those in Sections 13 to 16 may also usually be shown
in classes at shows for late-flowering types. Early-flowering
chrysanthemums (Sections 23 to 30) include all cultivars that
in a normal season bloom in the open ground before
1 October. Though these blooms must be grown in the open it
is usually permissible to protect them from weather damage.
It is permissible for canes, neatly tied, to be used to support
the stems of chrysanthemums of all sections. The supports
should be unobtrusive so as not to detract from the exhibit.

Sections 1 and 2
• Note: Rings may be used to support the blooms.
Merits   Reflexing types: a bloom in which the breadth and
depth are approximately equal and that has good shoulders
and a full centre. Florets (which may be either flat and broad
or quilled) gracefully reflexed, of good substance, fresh to the
tips, unspoiled and of bright colour. Incurving types: a bloom
that is globular or nearly so, with a full centre. Florets that are
broad incurved (either closely and regularly or loosely and
irregularly), fresh to the tips and of bright colour.
Defects   A bloom that is much broader than deep or lacks
good shoulders, is coarse or has a depressed centre. Florets that
are not gracefully reflexed, are of poor substance, stale (no
longer fresh) at the tips, spotted or of dull colour or drooping.
Points   *See pp116–117*

Sections 3, 13 and 23
Merits   A bloom that is compact and globular or nearly so.
Florets that are broad, smooth, rounded at the tips, of
sufficient length to form a graceful curve, closely and regularly
arranged, firm, fresh (including the outer ones) and of a clear,
decisive colour.
Defects   A bloom that is loose, flat, has a hollow centre or is
irregular in outline. Florets that are narrow, loosely or
irregularly arranged, soft, lacking freshness or of dull or
undecided colour.
•Note: No cups or rings are permissible but, in Section 3, the
stem may be supported.
Points   *See pp116–117*

Sections 4, 14 and 24
Merits   Blooms that are broad and deep and have full centres.
Florets of good substance, bright in colour and fresh to the tips.
Florets that reflex gracefully and overlap one another perfectly.
In types with quilled, sharply pointed florets that stand out
stiffly, freshness to the tips is of particular importance.
Defects   Blooms that are narrow or shallow or lack full

centres or have daisy-eyes, *ie* visible disc-florets. Florets that are of poor substance, stale, drooping, dull in colour, ragged or misplaced.
Points   *See pp116–117*

Section 5, 15 and 25
Merits   Blooms that are globular in outline, with breadth and depth approximately equal. Florets that are broad, incurving (either closely and regularly or loosely and irregularly), of good substance, fresh to the tips and of bright colour. In semi-reflexing types, a pleasing contrast in colour between the outer reflexing and the inner recurving florets.
Defects   Blooms that are too broad for their depth and not globular in outline. Florets that are narrow, of poor substance, stale or of dull colour.
Points   *See pp116–117*

Sections 6, 16 and 26
Merits   Blooms that have fresh, deep, symmetrical "cushions" (*ie* discs) of even size and bright colour. Ray-florets that are fresh and of bright colour: either broad to the tips, flat and of equal length or pointed and of uneven size.
Defects   Blooms with cushions that are stale, shallow, malformed, of uneven size or dull colour. Ray-florets that are drooping or not fresh to the tips or of a dull colour.
Points   *See pp116–117*

Sections 7, 17 and 27
Blooms with approximately five rows of ray-florets.
Merits   Flowers borne at right angles to the stems. Ray-florets that are broad, flat, of good substance, fresh to the tips and of a bright colour. Disc-florets that are fresh, clear and regular.
Defects   Flowers that are not borne at right angles to the stems. Ray-florets in excess or that are narrow, incurving or not flat or are of poor substance, drooping or stale. Disc-florets that are old, dull or irregular. Slight reflexing or incurving at the tips of ray-florets should be regarded as defective in some cultivars.
Points   *See pp116–117*

Sections 8, 18 and 28
Merits   Blooms that are symmetrical (ball-shaped), with full centres, of uniform size and bright colour.
Defects   Blooms that are asymmetrical, lack full centres, are of uneven size or of a dull colour.
Points   *See pp116–117*

Sections 9, 19 and 29

A spray for the purposes of these sections is the last flowering growth consisting of one stem (not a branch) with or without a central flower bud.

Merits The blooms of sprays should be fresh, clean, of uniform size, development and colour. Individual blooms evenly spaced and not overlapping one another. Foliage small, fresh and clean.

Defects Dead or faded blooms, colour variation and poor foliage.

Scales of points

Sections 3, 4, 5, 6, 7, 10, 11, 13, 14, 15, 16, 17, 20, 23, 24, 25, 26, 27 and 30, and sections 8, 9, 18, 19, 28 and 29 when shown as individual blooms

Form	6 points
Size	4 points
Freshness	4 points
Colour	2 points
Uniformity between blooms of a cultivar	2 points
Foliage	1 point
Staging	1 point
TOTAL	20 points

Sections 1 and 2

Form	5 points
Size	6 points
Freshness	6 points
Colour	2 points
Staging and foliage	1 point
TOTAL	20 points

Natural sprays from sections 8, 9, 18, 19, 28 and 29

Bloom quality:	Form	3 points
	Freshness	5 points
	Colour	3 points
Overall effect (including progression of development and staging)		8 points
Foliage		1 point
TOTAL		20 points

Exhibition sprays from sections 8, 9, 18, 19, 28 and 29

Bloom quality:	Form	3 points
	Freshness	4 points
	Colour	2 points
	Size	1 point
Spray quality:	Form	3 points
	Uniform placement and development	3 points
Overall effect (including staging and number of blooms)		3 points
Foliage		1 point
TOTAL		20 points

Chrysanthemums, specimen plants in pots

Merits A symmetrical plant, "facing all round", with a single main stem for not less than 25mm between the soil and the first branch or break. Blooms numerous and of high quality. Foliage ample, clean and healthy. Stems that have been bent gradually from near their bases. Supports and ties inconspicuous. There should be not less than 45mm of clear stem between soil level and the bottom of the head in standard pompons and not less than 60mm in standards of large-flowered cultivars.

Defects A plant that is not symmetrical or faces only one way or has more than one main stem immediately above the soil. Blooms that are not sufficiently numerous for the size of the plant or are lacking in quality. Stems that have been bent abruptly. Supports or ties that are obtrusive or ties too near the blooms.

Number, quality and freshness of blooms	10 points
Foliage	4 points
Training	6 points
TOTAL	20 points

Chrysanthemums, cascade

Merits A well-trained and balanced plant, evenly furnished with fully open blooms that are fresh and bright in colour. Training frames, canes and ties should be as inconspicuous as possible.

Defects A badly trained, unevenly balanced plant with few blooms open or with blooms past their best and fading. Training frames, canes and ties that are conspicuous or badly positioned.

Number, quality and freshness of blooms	8 points
Foliage	2 points
Training	10 points
TOTAL	20 points

Chrysanthemums, charm and cushion

Merits   A symmetrical plant "facing all round", evenly furnished with fully open blooms that are fresh and bright in colour. Foliage clean and healthy. Plant size commensurate with the size of the pot.

Defects   A plant that is not symmetrical or faces only one way, or is unevenly furnished with a low proportion of open blooms, or having flowers that are faded and dull. A loose open plant.

Number, quality and freshness of blooms	10 points
Foliage	4 points
Training	6 points
TOTAL	20 points

Daffodils (*Narcissus*)

Merits   Flower carried at nearly a right angle to the stem, except in species and hybrids where a pendent flower is typical, *eg Narcissus triandrus* and its hybrids. Perianth of smooth texture and good substance. Segments broad and overlapping from the base for a good proportion of their length, flat or slightly twisted symmetrically in each segment or in alternate segments. Corona or crown of good colour, texture and substance, proportionate to the perianth in length and width, any frill or flange at the brim being even and uniform. Stem straight and strong and proportionate in length to the size of the flower. Perianth and corona symmetrical. Neck of flower short. In double cultivars, segments and colour symmetrically arranged.

Defects   (*Note:* These defects would not necessarily apply to species.) A flower that is immature or over-mature, or in which the colours are faded or burnt, or in which the perianth or corona is not symmetrical. A flower or stem that shows signs of damage or disease. A flower that faces downwards, except in species and hybrids in which a pendent flower is typical. A perianth of poor or uneven colour, ribbed, thin or hooded. Segments that are too narrow to overlap for a good proportion of their length or that are neither flat nor symmetrically twisted, or that have notches, nicks or tears. A corona or crown of poor colour, texture or substance or that has a frill or flange that is uneven or has spots at the margin. A stem that is weak or bent and disproportionate in length to the flower. A long neck. In double cultivars, segments or colour unevenly distributed. A vase containing more than one stem in which the flowers are not uniform.

Allowances should be made if the class being judged permits containers of floriferous cultivars such as 'Carlton' or 'Ice Follies' to compete directly with shy-flowering species such as *N. watieri*.

Scale of points

The following scale should be used as a guide to the relative importance of the features of an exhibit. In classes for more than one vase, each vase should be judged and marked individually. Before this is done, the exhibit as a whole should be marked out of an additional 10 per cent of total points for visual impact and coverage of divisions and colour combinations. For example, in a class of six vases of single blooms judges should mark out of 10 for each vase, total 60 points, having first marked out of an additional 6 points (10 per cent) for impact of the group and diversity.

In a class for single blooms

Form and poise	3 points
Colour	2 points
Condition and texture	2 points
Stem	1 point
Size (for the cultivar)	1 point
Presentation	1 point
TOTAL	10 points

In a class with three or more blooms to a vase add 2 points for uniformity to the above.

In a class for daffodils exhibited in growth in pots, pans or bowls

Form, colour, size (for the cultivar), texture and poise of the blooms	4 points
Condition and cleanliness of the blooms and foliage	3 points
Impact, symmetry and uniformity	3 points
TOTAL	10 points

Classification

The following classification of daffodils has been adopted by the Royal Horticultural Society:

Division 1 Trumpet daffodils

One flower to a stem; corona (trumpet) as long as or longer than the perianth segments (petals).

Division 2 Large-cupped daffodils

One flower to a stem; corona (cup) more than one-third, but less than equal to the length of the perianth segments (petals).

Division 3 Small-cupped daffodils

One flower to a stem; corona (cup) not more than one-third the length of the perianth segments (petals).

Division 4 Double daffodils

One or more flowers to a stem, with doubling of the perianth segments or the corona or both.

Division 5 Triandrus daffodils

Characteristics of *N. triandrus* clearly evident: usually two or more pendent flowers to a stem; perianth segments reflexed.

Division 6 Cyclamineus daffodils

Characteristics of *N. cyclamineus* clearly evident: one flower to a stem; perianth segments significantly reflexed; flower at an acute angle to the stem, with a very short pedicel (neck).

Division 7 Jonquilla and Apodanthus daffodils

Characteristics of sections Jonquilla or Apodanthi clearly evident: one to five (rarely eight) flowers to a stem; perianth segments spreading or reflexed; corona cup-shaped, funnel-shaped or flared, usually wider than long; flowers usually fragrant.

Division 8 Tazetta daffodils

Characteristics of section Tazettae clearly evident: usually three to twenty flowers to a stout stem; perianth segments spreading, not reflexed; flowers usually fragrant.

Division 9 Poeticus daffodils

Characteristics of the *N. poeticus* group; usually one flower to a stem; perianth segments pure white; corona very short or disc-shaped, usually with a green and/or yellow centre and a red rim, but sometimes of a single colour; flowers usually fragrant.

Division 10 Bulbocodium daffodils

Characteristics of section Bulbocodium clearly evident; usually one flower to a stem; perianth segments insignificant compared with the dominant corona; anthers dorsifixed (attached more-or-less centrally to the filament); filament and style usually curved.

Division 11 Split-corona daffodils

Corona split, usually for more than half its length.

11a Collar daffodils have the corona segments opposite the perianth segments; the corona segments usually in two whorls of three.

11b Papillon daffodils have the corona segments alternate to the perianth segments; the corona segments usually in a single whorl of six.

Division 12 Other daffodils of garden origin
Daffodils which do not fit the definition of any other division.

Division 13 Daffodils distinguished solely by botanical name
Note: The characteristics for Divisions 5 to 10 are given for guidance only; they are not all necessarily expected to be present in every cultivar.

Intermediate and miniature
Intermediate daffodils: between 51 and 80mm in diameter
Miniature daffodils: up to 50mm in diameter

Perianth and corona colour
Where a class requires blooms to have a yellow-orange or white perianth or corona, the perianth or corona must be predominantly, but not necessarily exclusively, that colour

Rim
Rimmed daffodils are those which display at the corona rim a clearly defined band of colour that is different from the colour or colours of the corona base and mid-zone.

Dahlias
The following paragraphs were prepared in consultation with the National Dahlia Society (NDS).

Classification
The NDS produces a classified list of cultivars. A cultivar can only be shown in a class in which it is classified. NDS classifications are as follows:

Group 1	Single flowered	Group 7	Pompon
Group 2	Anemone-flowered	Group 8	Cactus
		Group 9	Semi-cactus
Group 3	Collerette	Group 10	Miscellaneous
Group 4	Waterlily-flowered	Group 11	Fimbriated
		Group 12	Single orchid (star)
Group 5	Decorative		
Group 6	Ball	Group 13	Double orchid

The 2007 edition of the *National Dahlia Society Classified Directory* has subdivided groups 4, 5, 8, 9 and 11 for show purposes as follows:

Giant:	over 260mm in diameter
Large:	between 220 and 260mm in diameter
Medium:	between 170 and 220mm in diameter
Small:	between 115 and 170mm in diameter
Miniature:	not exceeding 115mm in diameter

Group 6 is subdivided for show purposes as follows:

Small Ball:	between 115 and 170mm in diameter
Miniature Ball:	not exceeding 115mm in diameter

Group 7 Pompon: must not exceed 52mm in diameter

Merits Bloom fresh and clean, all florets intact, firm and without blemish or defect. Colour(s) clear and well-defined, and either consistent or evenly shaded or tipped throughout the bloom. The following standards may also be used when judging the different categories:

Single and Collerette Dahlias
Eight or more outer florets, possibly overlapping but not assuming double formation, equal in size, uniform in shape and formation, radiating evenly and regularly away from the central disc in a single flat plane with the outer edges rounded or pointed. Inner florets or collar of Collerettes not less than one third of the length of the outer florets, even in colour and formation. Central disc flat and circular, containing not more than two rows of pollen-bearing stamens. Bloom poised at an angle of not less than 45 degrees to the stem, which should be straight and proportionate to the size of the bloom.

Anemone-flowered Dahlias
Close and compact group of tubular florets comprising the centre of the bloom, circular in outline. Outer ray-florets equal in size, uniform in shape and formation, generally flat and regularly arranged around the central florets. Bloom poised at an angle of not less than 45 degrees to the stem, which should be straight and proportionate to the size of the bloom.

Waterlily Dahlias
Blooms should be fully double and the face view circular in outline and regular in arrangement. A firm, circular, closed centre, proportionate to the size of the flower. The depth of the bloom should be approximately half the diameter. Bloom poised at an angle of not less than 45 degrees to the stem,

which should be straight and of a length and thickness proportionate to the size of the bloom.

Decorative, Cactus and Semi-cactus Dahlias

Bloom symmetrical and outline perfectly circular. A firm, circular, closed centre, proportionate to the size of the flower. Bloom "full", having, without over-crowding, sufficient florets to prevent gaps in formation and outline and to give depth to the bloom, which should be approximately two-thirds, or more, of the diameter. Bloom poised at an angle of not less than 45 degrees to the stem, which should be straight and of a length and thickness proportionate to the size of the bloom. The formation of blooms and their florets should correspond to the standards laid down for that particular class of dahlia.

Ball Dahlias

Blooms should be ball-shaped but the tendency towards flatness on the face of the larger cultivars is acceptable. Ray-florets compact and dense at the centre, symmetrically arranged, dressing back to the stem to complete the ball shape of the bloom. Florets compact and dense at the centre. Bloom poised at an angle of not less than 45 degrees to the stem, which should be straight and of a length and thickness proportionate to the size of the bloom.

Pompon Dahlias

Bloom perfectly globular. Florets involute for the whole of their length, evenly and symmetrically arranged throughout the bloom and dressing back fully to the stem. Bloom facing upwards on a straight, firm stem.

Miscellaneous Dahlias

Blooms equal in size and uniform in formation. Bloom poised at an angle of not less than 45 degrees to the stem, which should be straight and proportionate to the size of the bloom.

Fimbriated Dahlias

Fully double blooms. Petals split or notched uniformly throughout the bloom, to create a fringed overall effect. Petals may be flat, involute, revolute, straight, incurving or twisted. Bloom poised at an angle of not less than 45 degrees to the stem, which should be straight and proportionate to the size of the bloom.

Single and Double orchid Dahlias

Blooms equal in size and uniform in formation. Bloom poised at an angle of not less than 45 degrees to the stem, which should be straight and proportionate to the size of the bloom.

Exhibits

An exhibit of dahlias should be so arranged that all the blooms face in the same direction, are clear of each other and a pleasant and balanced effect is achieved. Blooms should be staged with some dahlia foliage, preferably on the stem. The foliage should be clean, healthy and undamaged. The names of all cultivars in an exhibit should be clearly stated.

Defects   As a general principle anything that detracts from the perfection of a bloom, or an exhibit, is a fault and the seriousness or otherwise of the fault depends on the degree of imperfection. In judging an exhibit the following faults should be evaluated.

It is a very serious fault if a bloom is malformed, faces downwards, has been badly damaged, has limp drooping florets, has had an excessive number of florets removed, has an open (daisy-eyed) centre (double flowered cultivars only), has a centre that is hard and green, large and undeveloped or badly distorted, has a gap created by a missing outer floret (Groups 1–3 only), or seriously departs from the standard formation of the class of dahlia for which the class calls.

The following faults may be either minor or serious, in accordance with the amount by which the fault detracts from the perfection of a bloom: Oval, sunken or isolated centres, irregular or oval outline of bloom, uneven, irregular, or unbalanced formation, florets lacking freshness or bleached, discoloured, faded, eaten, bruised, malformed or otherwise blemished, where florets have been removed, stems that are bent, weak, short-jointed, thick or out of proportion, uneven or inconsistent colouring (except bicoloured blooms), shallow blooms, *ie* those lacking depth of fullness (except Groups 1, 3 and 4), blooms that are immature or past their best, or the presence of pests.

Angle of bloom (Group 7): the bloom of a pompon dahlia should face upwards on a straight, firm stem. Any variation should be regarded as a fault. When several blooms are shown together in an exhibit, it is a fault for them to face at different angles.

Disqualification must result for any of the following reasons:
1 Blooms of large-flowered dahlias exceeding 260mm;
   Blooms of medium-flowered dahlias exceeding 220mm;
   Blooms of small-flowered dahlias exceeding 170mm;
   Blooms of miniature-flowered dahlias exceeding 115mm;
   Blooms of pompon dahlias exceeding 52mm.

2 Blooms artificially supported above the top level of the vase.
3 Incorrect number of blooms in an exhibit, including buds
whether embryo or showing colour. All buds are treated as
blooms and will result in disqualification if not removed
over the correct number.
4 Classified blooms exhibited in wrong class. If a vase in a
multivase exhibit is NAS then the whole exhibit must be
disqualified. While the whole exhibit cannot be considered
for an award, awards to individual vases, other than the
disqualified vases, are permitted (*eg* best vase in its group in
that exhibit).

Pointing   The NDS does not favour the use of a scale of
points for judging. The Royal Horticultural Society considers
that in certain cases such a scale may provide a useful guide
and the following scale is accordingly suggested for use if
desired.

Form and centre	5 points
Condition	10 points
Stem	3 points
Colour	2 points
TOTAL	20 points

Delphiniums, spikes

Merits   Spikes that are in good condition. Long, tapering or
columnar in shape, with at least two thirds of florets open, and
staged with a minimum of 100mm of stem visible below the
bottom florets. Florets of good substance and colour, whether
of self, contrasting colour or striped, showing good placement.
Well-furnished florets of circular outline with neat and even
"eye" petals are preferred. Presentation is important, with
staging carried out to present an upright spike with clean
foliage inserted to conceal packing.

Defects   Unsatisfactory condition. Spikes that are underdeveloped, crooked or malformed, or that are sparsely or
irregularly furnished with florets, or are overcrowded. Florets
that are small, or that have faded or fallen petals. Signs of
stripped florets or conspicuous seed pods. Unsatisfactory
presentation.

Advice to judges   Delphinium spikes are preferably shown
with sideshoots removed.

Condition	5 points
Form and size of spike	5 points
Florets	5 points
Overall effect	5 points
TOTAL	20 points

Additional points in multivase classes:

Uniformity	3 points
TOTAL	23 points

Delphiniums, displayed florets

These should be presented as directed in the show schedule.
Merits *See Delphiniums, spikes.* Evenness is of added importance when florets only are displayed.
Defects *See Delphiniums, spikes*

Condition	5 points
Substance and clarity of colour	5 points
Size and uniformity	5 points
Presentation	5 points
TOTAL	20 points

Floral arrangements

Fashions in the design of such floral arrangements as baskets, vases, bowls, bouquets and dinner-table decorations change considerably from one period to another, as does the range of flowers and foliage used. Beauty of form and colour, lightness of arrangement, happy harmonies or suitable contrasts always meet with general approval. The use of suitable foliage, berries, fruits and seed pods, and accessories may be desirable and permitted or required by the schedule. The rarity and cost of the flowers should not, as such, influence judges.

The schedule will usually convey whether the class is interpretative or a straightforward arrangement, and may indicate whether the judges should be guided by rules and definitions formulated by:

National Association of Flower Arrangement Societies, Osborne House, 12 Devonshire Square, London EC2M 4TE.

Fuchsia blooms

Merits Flowers that are fully open and complete with all floral parts. All floral parts except the anthers should be free of pollen. The stigma should be fresh. The anthers should be at the stage of development where pollen is about to appear or has just appeared.

Defects Flowers that are dirty or damaged. Flowers that are not fully open, are incomplete or are immature. Flowers that have more or less than 4 sepals. Anthers that have lost their pollen. A stigma that has wilted or died.

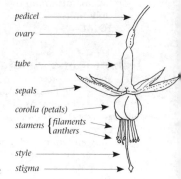

Parts of a fuchsia flower Diagram courtesy of the British Fuchsia Society

Advice to judges Check that each flower has 4 sepals, that each bloom is fresh and typical of the cultivar. Look for a well-balanced, clean exhibit with pollen on the anthers and with fresh stigmas.

Condition	4 points
Size (according to cultivar)	2 points
Colour	2 points
Presentation	2 points
TOTAL	10 points

Fuchsias

Merits A vigorous, symmetrical, floriferous plant, well furnished with clean and fresh blooms and foliage of good colour. Support and ties (if any) neat and unobtrusive. The length of clear stem from the soil to the lowest branch should be as follows: in a standard, not less than 750mm; in a half-standard, at least 450mm but less than 750mm; in a pyramid, not less than 25mm.

Defects A plant that is stunted, ill-balanced or sparsely flowered or that has poor or dirty foliage or has blooms that are not sufficiently open or past their best or that has untidy or obtrusive supports or ties or that has incorrect stem lengths for its group. A plant that shows evidence of insect injury or disease.

Quality and quantity of bloom	8 points
Quality and quantity of foliage	5 points
Cultural quality	5 points
Presentation	2 points
TOTAL	20 points

Gladiolus, Non-primulinus

Merits   An erect spike, with fresh, unblemished blooms and foliage. A long, well-balanced spike according to cultivar, still carrying the bottom flower and numerous other regularly spaced open and opening flowers and buds, so placed as to hide the stem and gradually narrowing from base to top. An ideal spike would be one third in full flower, one third with buds in colour and one third in green bud. Flowers that are typical of the cultivar and of good form, texture and colour.

Defects   A spike that is bent or has a drooping tip, or carries old or blemished flowers or empty bracts or a spike from which a bract has been removed or one with blemished foliage. A short, ill-balanced or crowded spike or one carrying few open flowers or flowers that are irregularly spaced or so placed that the stem is visible between them. Flowers that are small for the cultivar, of poor form, texture or colour.

Advice to judges   It is a serious fault for flowers to be removed from the spike.

Condition	6 points
Length and form of spike	5 points
Size, form and texture of flowers (for the cultivar)	5 points
Colour	4 points
TOTAL	20 points

Gladiolus, Primulinus type

Merits   An erect spike, with fresh unblemished blooms and foliage. Stem slender but strong, carrying 12 to 20 flowers and buds. Flowers openly, regularly and gracefully placed, facing forwards with one upper inside petal hooding over the central organs, the whole presenting a light appearance.

Defects   A bent or twisted spike, carrying old or blemished flowers or empty bracts. A spike from which a bract has been removed or with blemished foliage. Flowers tightly placed so as to hide the stem, not facing forward and without a hooded upper inside petal. Flowers not typical of the cultivar and heavy in general appearance.

Advice to judges   It is a serious fault for flowers to be removed from the spike.

Points   *As for Gladiolus, Non-primulinus, above*

Gourds, ornamental

Most gourds are small fruited, of various colours and colour patterns, warted or with other protuberances. A number of fruits will be required to demonstrate a range of the possibilities. The fruit should be displayed for effect on a dish or in a basket, to present a well-balanced and attractive display. Ornamental gourds must not be included in vegetable classes.

Merits   Fresh, fully developed, mature fruits with stalks attached, unvarnished, showing variation in colour and form and presenting a homogenous mixture.

Defects   Misshapen, immature, diseased or damaged fruit. Desiccated or over-yeared specimens or lacking a stalk. Large and small cultivars in the display.

Condition	4 points
Size, form and shape	4 points
Colour	4 points
TOTAL	12 points

Heathers

Merits   Good condition. Long, straight spikes of evenly spaced florets or large umbels with florets symmetrically arranged. Few unopened buds. No faded florets. Corollas undamaged. Foliage clean, bright-coloured and healthy.

Defects   Unsatisfactory condition. Spikes that are short, crooked or uneven, or thinly or irregularly furnished with flowers. Buds not yet open. Florets fading or turning brown. Corollas pierced by insects. Foliage that is dull, withered or unhealthy.

Condition	6 points
Spikes	6 points
Colour	4 points
Uniformity	4 points
TOTAL	20 points

Irises

The following is a general guide to judging iris classes. More detailed information about the many iris categories and guidelines for judging them can be obtained from the British Iris Society (www.britishirissociety.org.uk).

Merits Stems that are sturdy. Well-proportioned, fresh flowers of good colour. Clean foliage.

Defects Stems that are weak. Flowers that are damaged, unhealthy or fading. Blemished foliage.

Condition, including the number of flowers open at the time of judging	5 points
Colour	5 points
Stem and foliage	5 points
Quality of flower	5 points
TOTAL	20 points

Orchids

Merits A flower of good shape, substance and clear colour or combination of colours, commensurately large for the particular genus or for the specific parents. Numerous flowers in those genera that have more than one flower; not disbudded. Flowers complete, no parts missing. Where shown on a growing plant, as distinct from a cut-flower exhibit, the plant well grown and not made up of several pieces. A good plant of a species known to be difficult to grow.

Defects Flowers not fully open or damaged, unhealthy or fading. Flowers small for the genus, of poor shape, little substance and of poor colour. A plant that is poorly cultivated, blemished, diseased or otherwise damaged.

Condition	5 points
Flowers: Shape	6 points
Size	6 points
Substance	3 points
Colour	5 points
Difficulty of cultivation	5 points
TOTAL	30 points

Pansies, fancy (exhibition cultivars)

(See also Violas, p147)

Merits A flower that is large, fresh, clean, circular in outline, with smooth, thick, velvety petals without serrations, lying evenly on each other and either flat or slightly reflexed so that the surface of the flower is slightly convex. Centre petals that meet above the eye and reach well up on the top petals and a bottom petal that is sufficiently deep and broad to balance the others. Colours that are harmonious; belting (margin) of uniform width; blotches that are large, solid, rounded and clearly defined; and an eye that is bright yellow, solid, circular and well defined.

Defects A flower that is less than 63mm in diameter, is past its best, soil marked, concave or lacking a circular outline. Petals that are fishtailed, thin, of poor substance or serrated. Belting (margin) that is very narrow or more than 8.4mm wide or of uneven width or ill-defined; blotches that are small, thin or ragged-edged; an eye that is dull or ill-defined.

Condition	3 points
Form and texture	5 points
Size	3 points
Colour	3 points
Belting	2 points
Blotch	2 points
Eye	2 points
TOTAL	20 points

Pansies, show

(See also Violas, p147)

Merits A flower that is between 38mm and 50mm in diameter, fresh and clean and with the same form, build, texture and eye as in a fancy pansy.

A bicolour flower with a ground-colour of the same shade throughout, circular, broad, of uniform width and well defined at its edge. Belting (margin) of uniform width, of exactly the same colour as the top petals, distinct from the ground-colour and well defined at its junction with the ground-colour. A blotch of good size (though smaller than in a fancy pansy), dense, solid and approximately circular.

In a "dark self-coloured" flower: the same shade throughout with no trace of a blotch. In any other "self-coloured" flower: the same shade throughout except for a blotch as in a bicolour.

Defects A flower that is less than 38mm or over 50mm in diameter, past its best, soil marked, concave or lacking a circular outline. Petals that are fishtailed, thin or of poor substance or serrated. Belting (margin) that is very narrow or very wide, of uneven width or ill-defined or not of the same colour as the top petals or not distinct from the ground-colour. Except in a "dark self-coloured" flower, a blotch that is small, thin or ragged-edged. An eye that is dull or ill-defined.

Points   *As for Pansies, fancy (exhibition cultivars), p132.*

Pansies, fancy (garden cultivars)

(See also **Violas,** *p147)*

Judging characteristics for this group should closely follow those for the exhibition cultivars. However, it should be noted that as garden cultivars are generally raised from seed each year, there will be a greater degree of variation than found among the exhibition types, named cultivars of which are reproduced vegetatively.

Merits   A flower that is large, clean and fresh, approaching in most respects the desirable qualities of the exhibition fancy pansy. Uniformity in the size, form and symmetry of markings (blotch and margins), though these may differ in their proportions compared with what is demanded of an exhibition cultivar.

Defects   A flower that is less than 35mm diameter, that is past its best, soil marked, concave or lacking a circular outline. Petals of poor substance, a blotch that is lacking density or ill-defined edges. A V-shaped gap between the middle petals. The top edge of the bottom petal sloping sharply downwards. An ill-defined eye that runs into the blotch.

Points   *As for Pansies, fancy (exhibition cultivars), p132.*

Pelargoniums, ivy-leaved

Merits   A floriferous plant of pleasing form. Ample, healthy, clean and bright foliage. Well-developed trusses. A bright, clear and distinct colour.

Defects   A plant that is of unpleasing form or is partly defoliated or has insufficient flowers. Leaves that are coarse, yellowing, dull or dirty, or that show evidence of insect injury or disease. Trusses that are not fully developed.

Cultural quality	6 points
Trusses	8 points
Foliage	3 points
Presentation	3 points
TOTAL	20 points

Pelargoniums, zonal and regal

Merits A shapely plant, proportionate to the size of the pot. Trusses should be proportionate in number to the size of the plant and of bright, clear and distinct colour. Large, round flowers (pips) with broad overlapping petals.

Defects A misshapen or partly defoliated plant, with too few trusses for its size. Trusses that are small, thin, or have too few fully expanded flowers (pips) or have weak stems. Leaves that are coarse, yellowing or dirty, or that show evidence of insect injury or disease.

Cultural quality	6 points
Trusses	8 points
Foliage	3 points
Presentation	3 points
TOTAL	20 points

Pinks

Singles must have five evenly shaped flat petals at right angles to the stem, or five evenly shaped, waved petals which need not be at right angles to the stem. In both cases the petals should overlap.

Doubles consist of all other pinks that are not single, irrespective of the number of petals.

Pinks may be classed according to colour as follows:
Selfs, which must be of one clear colour.
Bi-colours, which must have two colours in concentric zones on every petal; the boundary between the colours should be clear.
Fancies, which may have any ground-colour and be marked or suffused with another contrasting colour or colours on every petal.
Laced Pinks, which may be double, or single with five petals, with unbroken laced markings on every petal.

Merits Good condition. Flowers that are symmetrical, circular in outline and appear light and dainty. Petals that are of good substance, flat and with edges either smooth or regularly serrated. Guard-petals broad and at right angles to the calyx. In double pinks, inner petals that are evenly disposed, diminishing in size toward the centre. Calyx not split. Stems that are rigid, supporting the flowers so that they face upward or at a slight angle, and carrying subsidiary blooms or buds. Clear, bright, colours and well-defined markings, if any. A strong scent. Glaucous foliage. Uniformity.

Defects   Unsatisfactory condition. Flowers that are
asymmetrical, not circular in outline, or appearing coarse.
Petals that are of poor substance or ribbed. Guard-petals that
are narrow or are incurved or recurved. Inner petals of double
pinks that are not evenly disposed. Calyx split. Stems not
rigid, with flowers that face downward, or that carry no
subsidiary blooms or buds. Poor colours or ill-defined
markings. Lack of fragrance. Lack of uniformity. Unless
specifically permitted by the schedule, exhibits with supports
to the stems or calyx-bands should be disqualified.

Condition	7 points
Form	7 points
Colour	3 points
Size (for cultivar)	3 points
TOTAL	20 points

Polyanthus
Merits   Good condition, including healthy, undamaged
foliage and flowers. Long, stout, erect flower stems. Large,
compact, symmetrical trusses. Large, circular, flat pips of good
substance. Bright colours.
Defects   A plant in poor condition or with unhealthy or
damaged foliage or flowers. Flower stems that are short, weak
or not erect. Trusses that are small or loose or have such short
pedicels that the pips overlap unduly. Pips that are small,
starry, not flat or of poor substance.

Condition	5 points
Flower stems	4 points
Trusses	4 points
Pips	4 points
Colour	3 points
TOTAL	20 points

Pot plants and house plants
**(other than those for which separate criteria are given
elsewhere in this section)**
Pots or containers should be clean and undamaged and where
staking, tying or wiring is necessary, it should be neatly done
in a manner that does not detract from the appearance of
the plant.

Ferns, bromeliads and orchids and similar plants that are
naturally epiphytic may be shown attached to a piece of bark
or wood instead of in pots and should not be disqualified in a
pot-plant class simply because they are not shown with their
roots inside a container.

Plants usually grown for their ornamental foliage may not be debarred from foliage plant classes simply because they happen to be in flower at the time of the competition but, if in flower, they must also be considered eligible for entry in flowering-plant classes. Judges must consider only the attribute called for in the wording of the class and, if they are judging a foliage class, must take no account of any flowers on a plant, while, when judging a flowering-plant class, they must only award points for foliage on the usual scale. For show purposes the highly coloured ornamental bracts on plants such as *Bougainvillea*, *Euphorbia* and *Justicia* (*Beloperone*) are considered to be an integral part of the flower and do not qualify for consideration as foliage in pot plant classes.

Where it is usual to grow a number of corms, tubers, cuttings or bulbs in a pot to give a well-furnished appearance (*eg Achimenes*, *Tradescantia* or *Freesia*) the pot is admissible as "a pot plant" even though there is, strictly speaking, more than one plant in the container.

Flowering or fruiting plants

Merits   A sturdy, shapely plant, well furnished with healthy, unblemished foliage and flowers, displaying flowers, coloured bracts or fruits of good size, colour and substance. Preference should be given to decorative rather than botanical value but, other things being equal, the greater degree of skill required to produce certain plants to perfection should be taken into consideration.

Defects   A drawn, undernourished plant with unhealthy, deformed, undersized, scanty or diseased foliage and flowers with undersized flowers, bracts or fruits of poor substance and dull, ill-defined colours. A plant that is easy to grow if in competition with one that is difficult to grow.

Advice to judges   Most flowering and fruiting pot plants should be shown for all-round effect but others such as orchids, large-flowered begonias, etc should not be downpointed if they do not possess this attribute.

Condition	6 points
Quality and quantity of bloom or fruit	6 points
Cultivation	5 points
Difficulty of cultivation	3 points
TOTAL	20 points

Foliage plants (decorative in form and/or colour)

Merits   A sturdy, shapely plant, well furnished with clean, unblemished, healthy foliage. Though preference should be given to decorative value, all other things being equal, the greater degree of skill required to produce certain plants to perfection should be taken into consideration.

Defects A drawn, undernourished plant with unhealthy, deformed, undersized, scanty or diseased foliage, of little ornamental value. A plant that is easy to grow if in competition with one that is difficult to grow.

Advice to judges The presence of flowers on a foliage plant should not be considered a fault but the decorative value of the flowers should be disregarded.

Condition	6 points
Decorative value	6 points
Cultivation	5 points
Difficulty of cultivation	3 points
TOTAL	20 points

Primroses

Merits A tufted and compact habit of growth. Foliage and flowers that are healthy and undamaged. Numerous flowers, produced singly on long peduncles and forming a symmetrical mass. Flowers of good substance, circular in outline with definite, clear colours.

Defects A plant with a loose habit of growth or with unhealthy or blemished foliage or flowers. Flowers that are few or have short stalks or are not arranged symmetrically or are of poor substance or are not circular in outline.

Condition	6 points
Floriferousness	5 points
Flowers	6 points
Colour	3 points
TOTAL	20 points

Primula species including *P. malacoides*, *P. obconica* and *P. sinensis* type

Merits   A vigorous plant with foliage undamaged and free from blemish and that carries numerous open flowers. Trusses with strong stems, carrying the flowers well above the foliage. Flowers well formed, of good substance and with fresh, clear colours.

Defects   A plant that is drawn or weak or has damaged or blemished foliage or few flowers or is ill-balanced. Trusses that are small or that do not carry the flowers above the foliage. Flowers that are of poor substance.

Condition	6 points
Trusses	5 points
Flowers	6 points
Colour	3 points
TOTAL	20 points

Rock-garden plants
See Alpine-house and rock-garden rlants, p107

Roses, general
The following paragraphs summarise the Royal National Rose Society (RNRS) rules and were prepared in consultation with the RNRS.

Notes
Large flowered, cluster flowered: for exhibition purposes the expressions 'large flowered' and 'cluster flowered' apply wherever appropriate to all divisions of modern garden roses, not just modern repeat-flowering bush roses. Whatever the type, the exhibit must meet the standards applicable to the class in which the exhibit is entered.

Stem: an original new growth with no lateral growth present and one that has not been 'stopped'. Stems with lateral growth removed should not be downpointed. Stems with lateral growth present, or where growth has been stopped, should be downpointed by 3 points per stem. Disbudding and deadheading are permitted under this rule.

Double blooms: blooms with more than 20 petals.

Semi-double blooms: blooms with between 8 and 20 petals.

Single blooms: blooms with less than 8 petals.

Side buds: these are permitted in all large flowered classes except those for Specimen Blooms and for Three Stage Roses. No more than 3 buds/blooms per stem are permitted under this rule.

Foliage: unless expressly permitted by the schedule, the insertion of any additional foliage disqualifies an exhibit. The 'dressing' of foliage by the use of anything other than plain water is not permitted.

Merits
• **Individual bloom:** Double blooms in the 'perfect stage' should be half to three-quarters open with the petals symmetrically arranged within a circular outline.

For any Large Flowered (HT) type, the outer petals should regularly surround an upright and well-formed conical and pointed centre. For any other type the outer petals should regularly surround a central formation typical of the cultivar, *eg* rounded, rosette, quartered, pompon, etc.

Double blooms in the 'full bloom' stage should be fully open with the petals symmetrically arranged within a circular outline; the stamens, if exposed, should be fresh and of good colour.

Single and semi-double blooms in the 'perfect' or 'full bloom' stage (often indistinguishable) should have petals that are symmetrically arranged within a circular outline and the stamens, if exposed, should be fresh and of good colour.

Any type in the 'bud stage' should show full colour with one or two petals beginning to unfurl above an opening calyx.

Any type in the 'hip stage' should have fruit that is fully developed and of the typical size, shape and colour of a ripe hip of the cultivar.
• **Cluster:** Two or more blooms. The inflorescence should be representative of its cultivar with the blooms gracefully arranged and so spaced as to permit their natural development, neither being crushed together nor exposing wide gaps between them.

Note: this does not apply to large flowered roses.
• **Substance:** This refers to the petals which should be firm, smooth and of good texture, neither coarse nor flimsy and free from blemish.
• **Size of individual bloom:** The bloom should be of good average size for a well-grown plant of the particular cultivar. Except in classes for 'specimen blooms', where size is important irrespective of cultivar, a bloom of above-average size should not be regarded as being of special merit.
• **Freshness of bloom:** Appearance should be sparkling and clean with no suggestion of tiredness, staleness or unnatural preservation.
• **Brilliance of colour:** The colour should be bright and glowing, not dull or faded.
• **Purity of colour:** The bloom should display the full depth of

the true seasonal colour of the cultivar, with no suggestion of deviation, blueing or tarnishing.

• **Stem:** The stem should be straight and proportionate in thickness and length to the size of the bloom it supports, being neither unduly thin and spindly nor coarsely thick and clumsy.

• **Foliage:** Adequate in quantity and size; undamaged, fresh and clean in appearance, of good colour and substance for the cultivar and with no evidence of the use of artificial aids to enhance appearance.

Note: stem and foliage standards are not applied when judging 'specimen blooms' in boxes.

• **Presentation:** The exhibit should be balanced in height and width in relation to the container, and enhanced by good colour combination. The flowers and foliage should be artistically arranged to avoid either crushing or excessive gaps and without exposing such expanses of stem or foliage that the flowers are not the dominant feature of the exhibit. In exhibits comprising numbers of individual blooms (typically boxes, bowls, palettes or vases of specimen and miniature roses) the blooms should be uniform in size, state of development and freshness. The overall shape of basket exhibits should follow the contours of the basket and permit the theoretical use of the handle.

• **Roses grown and staged in pots or other containers:** It is important to note the difference between 'a rose grown in a pot or container' and 'a pot or container of roses'. In the former, only one plant is required whilst in the latter a number of plants is permissible. The plants should be representative of well-grown specimens of the cultivar and present a well-balanced exhibit.

Defects

Individual blooms of irregular outline; having fewer than average number of petals; split, blunt or confused centres; stained or damaged petals; evidence of removal or trimming of petals; immaturity or over-development of blooms; over-dressing so as to appear unnatural; blooms left tied or pelleted.

Clusters with poor outline, blooms irregularly placed; crushed tightly together or so widely spaced as to show gaps; a high proportion of unopened buds or aged blooms; hips or stalks of spent blooms left showing.

Poor substance of petals; flimsy and drooping or rough, coarse, creased or diseased.

Size not representative of a well-grown example of the cultivar.

Blooms that do not appear to be sparkling fresh; giving an

impression of being tired, drawn, stale or wan.

Dull or faded colour. Deviation from true colour of a well-grown example of the cultivar, excessive white streaking, dark or tarnished markings, blueing (especially of red roses.)

Stems weak, twisted, bent, flattened in section, unduly thick in relation to the blooms carried, marked, diseased or damaged.

Poor, thin foliage, inadequate in size or quantity; of bad colour, misshapen, misplaced, diseased or damaged.

Untidy presentation; unpleasant overall effect, lopsided appearance, obtrusive wiring (where wiring is permitted), excessive or inadequate length of stem in relation to the size and number of blooms carried; exhibit too tall and narrow or too flat and wide; flowers or clusters crushed together or too widely spaced; poor colour balance; excessive display of stems and/or foliage so that the flowers are not the dominant feature of the exhibit; dirty containers or boxes.

Roses, except specimen blooms, three stage roses and miniature roses

Merits   *As for Roses, general*

Defects   *As for Roses, general*

Advice to judges   Each receptacle is considered as a separate unit. Thus, in a class for 1 vase or bowl, 20 points is the maximum possible score while, in a class for 3 vases each vase is assessed out of 20 points so that 60 points is the maximum possible score for an exhibit. In classes that specify a minimum and/or maximum number of cultivars, blooms or stems, the number actually staged may be taken into consideration as an additional criterion (excluding any stems that have been downpointed). If blooms are left tied or pelleted, up to 3 points must be deducted for each bloom so left in each receptacle. Blooms so overdressed as to alter their character must be regarded as very seriously defective and up to 3 points per bloom must be deducted.

Form and size of individual bloom(s), form of cluster(s), substance	5 points
Freshness, brilliance, purity of colour	5 points
Stems and foliage	3 points
Presentation	7 points
TOTAL	20 points

Roses, specimen blooms other than those in bowls or vases

Merits *As for Roses, general,* except the merits for cluster, stem and foliage which do not apply. A bloom of above-average size for a large flowered rose, irrespective of cultivar, is desirable provided this is not achieved at the expense of other criteria.

Defects *As for Roses, general,* except the defects for cluster, stem and foliage which do not apply.

Advice to judges It is important to note that, while each bloom is awarded points for quality and size individually, for presentation the points are awarded per unit of 6 blooms. Thus a box of 6 specimen blooms may earn 5 points for presentation, a box of 12 may earn 10 points and so on. If blooms are left tied or pelleted, up to 3 points must be deducted for each bloom so left in each receptacle. Blooms so overdressed as to alter their character must be regarded as very seriously defective and up to 3 points per bloom must be deducted.

> **Form and size of individual bloom,**
> **substance, freshness, brilliance,**
> **purity of colour (for each bloom)   5 points**

For an exceptional bloom, 1 or even 2 extra points may be awarded

> **Presentation (for each unit of 6 blooms)   5 points**

Roses, specimen blooms in bowls or vases

Merits *As for Roses, general,* except the merit for cluster which does not apply. A bloom of above-average size for a large-flowered rose, irrespective of cultivar, is desirable provided that this is not achieved at the expense of other relevant merits.

Defects *As for Roses, general,* except the defect for cluster which does not apply.

Advice to judges In classes that specify a minimum and/or maximum number of cultivars or blooms, the number actually staged may be taken into consideration as an additional criterion (excluding any stems that have been downpointed). If blooms are left tied or pelleted, up to 3 points must be deducted for each bloom so left in each receptacle. Blooms so overdressed as to alter their character must be regarded as very seriously defective and up to 3 points per bloom must be deducted.

Form and size of individual bloom(s),
substance, freshness, brilliance,
purity of colour (for each bloom)   5 points

For an exceptional bloom, 1 or even 2 extra points may
be awarded

Stems and foliage (for each exhibit)   3 points
Presentation (for each exhibit)   5 points

Three stage roses

3 blooms of one cultivar: one in the bud stage, one in the
perfect stage, and one in the full bloom stage (refer to *Roses,
General, Notes* for further details of these stages).

Merits   *As for Roses, general*

Defects   *As for Roses, general*

Advice to judges   The bud should be showing its full colour,
with one or two petals beginning to unfurl above an opening
calyx. The perfect-stage bloom should be of average size for
the cultivar, half to three quarters open with the petals
symmetrically arranged within a circular outline. The full
bloom should be of average size for the cultivar and should be
fully open with the petals arranged within a circular outline;
the stamens, if exposed, should be fresh and of a good colour.
Each stem must be of the same cultivar. If blooms are left tied
or pelleted, up to 3 points must be deducted for each bloom so
left in each receptacle. Blooms so overdressed as to alter their
character must be regarded as very seriously defective and up
to 3 points per bloom must be deducted.

Form and size of individual blooms, substance	5 points
Freshness, brilliance, purity of colour	5 points
Stems and foliage	3 points
Presentation	7 points
TOTAL	20 points

Miniature roses in bowls, baskets and vases

Merits   *As for Roses, general.* In addition, miniature roses should be miniature in all aspects of size of flowers, foliage and stems. All types of miniature roses are eligible but they must be representative of their cultivar and conform to the requirements of the schedule. Foliage should be representative of the cultivar and in reasonable proportion to the size of the blooms. In classes for bowls, baskets and vases, the exhibit must be balanced in relation to the container and arranged and spaced so as to permit the natural development of the blooms, neither being crushed together nor exposing wide gaps between stems or individual blooms. All exhibits should be presented with an emphasis on the daintiness appropriate to miniature roses.

Defects   *As for Roses, general*

Advice to judges   In awarding points, each receptacle is considered as a separate unit. Thus, in a class for 1 vase or bowl, 20 points is the maximum possible score while, in a class for 3 vases, each vase is assessed out of 20 points so that 60 points is the maximum possible score for an exhibit. In classes that specify a minimum and/or maximum number of cultivars, blooms or stems, the number actually staged may be taken into consideration as an additional criterion (excluding any stems that have been downpointed). If blooms are left tied or pelleted, up to 3 points must be deducted for each bloom so left in each receptacle. Blooms so overdressed as to alter their character must be regarded as very seriously defective and up to 3 points per bloom must be deducted.

Form and size of individual bloom(s), form of cluster(s), substance and stage of development	5 points
Freshness, brilliance, purity of colour	5 points
Stems and foliage	3 points
Presentation	7 points
TOTAL	20 points

Miniature roses in boxes, palettes and similar

Merits   *As for Miniature roses in bowls, baskets and vases*. The merits for clusters, stem and foliage do not apply. The blooms should be of average size for the cultivar and should be presented in the 'perfect' stage in boxes, and in the 'full bloom' stage in palettes. In palettes colour placement of blooms is especially important, the criterion being a well-balanced exhibit of individual miniature rose blooms at their best.

Defects   *As for Roses, general*

Advice to judges   Blooms are to be contained within the confines of the box or palette and must not overlap (although petals may touch). In the case of blooms not meeting this criterion, up to 3 points per bloom must be deducted. It is important to note that while each bloom is awarded points for quality and size individually, above-average size is not considered meritorious. For presentation the points are awarded per unit of 6 or 7 blooms. Thus a box of 6 blooms may earn 5 points for presentation, a box of 12 may earn 10 points and so on. If blooms are left tied or pelleted, up to 3 points must be deducted for each bloom so left in each receptacle. Blooms so overdressed as to alter their character must be regarded as very seriously defective and up to 3 points per bloom must be deducted.

Form and size of individual bloom, substance, freshness, brilliance, purity of colour (for each bloom)	5 points
Presentation (for each unit of 6 or 7 blooms)	5 points

Three stage miniatures

See Three stage roses, p143

Sweet peas

Merits   Strong spikes with well-spaced blooms, each one fully open and fresh. Large flowers with erect standards, rigid wings and keel closed, free from colour-running, spotting or scorching and of a bright colour with a silken sheen. Long, straight stems in proportion to the size of the blooms. Effectiveness of staging (particularly when competition is close).

Defects   Weak spikes with irregularly placed blooms or having undeveloped or poorly coloured top blooms or with blooms showing seed pods or losing colour. Flowers small for the cultivar, malformed, spotted, scorched or with poor or running colour. Stems crooked or disproportionately short or long for the size of the blooms. Stems with fewer than four flowers.

Freshness, cleanliness and condition	7 points
Form, placement and uniformity	6 points
Trueness of colour	4 points
Size of bloom in balance with stem	3 points
TOTAL	20 points

Tulips (other than English florist)

All tulips with the exception of those in the Single and Late Double and Parrot Groups must have six petals and six filaments with anthers. Any exhibit containing flowers that have more or less than this number would not be disqualified, but would only receive an award in the absence of acceptable exhibits. Any exhibit containing flowers that are clearly diseased as a result of tulip breaking virus will not be considered for an award. No artificial support or wiring of blooms is allowed.

Merits   Flowers in good condition, in their most perfect phase and unblemished, of a good colour for the cultivar, of firm substance and smooth texture and of the form typical of the group to which the cultivar belongs. Stems that are stiff and strong enough to support the flowers, with attached foliage that is stiff and in good condition.

Defects   Flowers immature or past their perfect phase, spotted, blistered or otherwise blemished, of poor colour for the cultivar, thin, of rough texture or not of the form typical of their group. Stems limp or too weak to support the flowers, with foliage that is limp or very badly blemished.

Advice to judges   Where there are a number of flowers in a vase then uniformity of size and form is very important and a maximum of five additional points should be awarded in a class calling for three to six blooms, and a maximum of ten points for nine to 18 blooms.

Condition	4 points
Form	4 points
Colour	4 points
Size (for the cultivar)	2 points
Substance	3 points
Stems and attached foliage	3 points
TOTAL	20 points

Violas (exhibition cultivars)

(See also Pansies, fancy (exhibition cultivars), pp132–133)

Merits   A flower that is large, fresh, clean and of the form, build and texture outlined for fancy pansies *(see pp132–133)*. While the colour may be self, striped, mottled, suffused or belted (margined), there must be no semblance of a blotch or any rays and the eye must be bright, solid, circular and well defined.

Defects   A flower that is less than 63mm in diameter, past its best, soil marked, concave or lacking a circular outline. Petals fishtailed or with V-shaped gaps between them or thin, of poor substance or serrated. Any semblance of a blotch or of rays. An eye that is very large or is square or ill-defined.

Condition	3 points
Form and texture	5 points
Size	3 points
Colour	7 points
Eye	2 points
TOTAL	20 points

Violas (garden cultivars)

(See also Pansies, p133)

Merits   A flower that is clean, fresh and of good substance. Circular or oval in form without trace of blotch or ray. An eye that is well defined, circular and a bright yellow or orange. Selfs have a clear and distinct ground colour. Margined flowers have well-defined edges of contrasting colour. Fancy, striped or suffused flowers show a pleasing or striking contrast.

Defects   A flower that is less than 25mm or more than 50mm in diameter, past its best, soil marked, lacking a circular or oval form. Petals of poor substance with dull or faded colour. Any semblance of blotch or ray, or gaps between petals. A large or square eye that runs into the ground colour.

Points   *As for Violas (exhibition cultivars), above.*

THE JUDGING OF GARDENS AND ALLOTMENTS

The inspection of gardens and allotments in competition with each other should be timed so that a comprehensive assessment of the ornamental or productive value throughout the whole of the year may be made rather than simply judging the entry at its peak. This will normally require the judges to make at least two visits, one in June or the first week in July and another between mid-August and mid-September. Where possible all entries in the competition should be assessed within a maximum period of five days.

The days for judging should be fixed by the competition's organising committee in consultation with the judges, and competitors should be given an indication of when their garden or allotment is likely to be visited.

Competition organisers should ensure that the judge is accompanied by a steward who knows the exact location of all the entrants and has copies of their official entries.

1 The judging of gardens

Contemporary domestic gardens fall within three broad categories.

Amenity gardens with less than 20% devoted to the production of fruit and/or vegetables.

Dual-purpose gardens with between 20 and 50% devoted to the production of fruit and/or vegetables as well as a substantial amenity area.

Utility gardens in which more than 50% is devoted to the production of fruit and/or vegetables and only a small space reserved for amenity or ornamental purposes.

In the judging of gardens credit should be given to the best use of the space, the quality of the plants including grassed areas, design and the intelligent placing of plants in suitable locations and aspects. The overall size of the garden should not be taken into account nor should the diversity or lack of diversity of plants. A limited number of healthy, well-grown plants making the best use of the space available is more meritorious than a wide variety of plants poorly grown and overcrowded or sparsely planted. Brown patches in lawns where the spent foliage of spring bulbs such as daffodils or crocuses has recently been mown off must not be considered a demerit. The relative immaturity of some trees or shrubs should not, in itself, be considered a demerit provided that the plant is appropriately sited and, where necessary, properly staked and/or protected.

The following pointing systems are offered as a guide but competition organisers may wish to adapt them to suit their own specific circumstances; where such adaptations are made, the judges should be advised of them when they are invited to judge.

Amenity gardens

Health, vigour and suitability of plants	100 points
Suitability of design to its site and usage	75 points
Maintenance of paths, structures, lawns and other grassed areas and working areas	50 points
Cultivation and freedom from perennial weeds	50 points
Harmonious blending of colours, shapes and textures	75 points
TOTAL	**350 points**

Dual-purpose gardens

Health, vigour and suitability of plants in both amenity and kitchen garden areas	100 points
Maintenance of paths, structures, lawns and grassed areas and working areas	50 points
Range and cultivation of plants in the kitchen garden area	75 points
Design and co-ordination of colours, shapes and textures in the amenity area	75 points
Overall integration of the two elements into a single, attractive, practical whole.	50 points
TOTAL	**350 points**

Utility gardens

Health, vigour, cultivation and arrangement of vegetables, and/or flowers, and/or fruit and/or culinary herb crops	150 points
Planning for regular rotations, and successional plantings to give optimum use of space, year-round produce and to minimise the build-up of pests and soil borne diseases	75 points
Maintenance of paths, crops, supports, cloches, frames and other structures	45 points
Utilisation of boundary walls or fences or other supports for training soft or top fruits or climbing vegetables	45 points
Neatness, practicality, planting and design of amenity area and the suitability of its siting within the overall garden area	35 points
TOTAL	**350 points**

Alternatively the following pointing system may be used:

Vegetable gardens

Section 1 Cultivation (cropping scheme, quality
of work, cleanliness, stored humus
or compost heap).   25 points

Section 2 For potatoes, 12; winter brassicas, 12;
onions, 12; carrots, 12; celery, 8; leeks,
8; beetroot, 6; parsnips, 5   75 points

Section 3 For peas, 12; runner or climbing beans,
12; summer brassicas, 12; lettuces, 8;
tomatoes, 8; broad beans, 6; dwarf French
beans, 6; vegetable marrows, 6   70 points

Section 4 For any other kinds of vegetable not
mentioned above (including salads),
3 points each kind; not more than
six kinds to receive points in final total.   18 points

TOTAL   **188 points**

Flower gardens

Section 1 For general scheme, 30; tasteful arrangement, 20; cultivation and cleanliness, 20   70 points

Section 2 For shrubs and trees, climbers, rock
garden, lawn, paths, greenhouse, fences
and hedges: 8 each, but only four of
these to receive marks   32 points

Section 3 For hardy herbaceous perennials,
annuals and biennials, roses, tender
plants, windowboxes, window plants,
etc: 8 each, but only four of these to
receive marks.   32 points

Section 4 For special features   16 points

TOTAL   **150 points**

Glasshouses, frames and other protected areas

Section 1 Standard of cultivation, 15; utilisation
of growing space, 10; cleanliness, 5   30 points

Section 2 For tomatoes, 10; cucumbers, 10;
aubergines, 10; peppers, 10; fruit, 10;
but only three of these to receive marks.   30 points

Section 3 Ornamental pot plants   20 points

Section 4 Other plants, 5; specialist collections, 15 20 points

TOTAL   **100 points**

Fruit gardens

The garden should contain not less than six kinds of fruits.

Section 1 For the overall planting scheme 12;
good pruning, training, tree and bush
form and plant supports 12; cultivation,
cleanliness, pest and disease control 12   36 points

Section 2 For apples, 12; pears, 10; plums, 10;
grapes, 10; cherries, 8; currants, black, 8;
currants, other than black, 8; gooseberries, 8;
raspberries, 8; strawberries, 8; blackberries,
or hybrid berries, 8   98 points

(The tree and bush fruits to consist of at least two plants of
any one kind, grapes one, blackberries and/or hybrid berries
two, strawberries 4m of row and raspberries 4m length of row.)

Section 3 For peach and/or nectarine fan trained, 10; in bush
form, 8; fig fan trained, 10   28 points

Section 4 For any other kind of fruit not mentioned above 4
points each kind, not more than four kinds to
receive points in final total.   16 points

TOTAL   **178 points**

2 The judging of allotments

For competition purposes an allotment is considered to be an
area of land separate from and in addition to the household
garden adjacent to the owner's property; or a plot cultivated
by a householder who has no garden as part of his/her own
domestic premises.

The primary purpose of an allotment is to provide crops of
vegetables, fruit, flowers and culinary herbs for household use
and the more completely a plot fulfils this objective the greater
should be the credit accorded to it in competition.

Allotments also allow enthusiasts for one particular plant
or group of plants to indulge their particular passion and a
plot given over to the monoculture of, say, dahlias or
carnations must be judged according to the standard and
quality of cultivation.

The size of plot should not be a factor for consideration in
competition but where there are a great many entries of
varying sizes organisers should consider dividing the competition into three or four separate classes according to size.

The following pointing systems are offered as a guide but competition organisers may wish to adapt these to suit local conditions or requirements.

Condition of the plot   **60 points**
Plots should be well stocked with crops free from obvious signs of excessive damage by pests, disease or weather. Any unplanted areas where crops have just been harvested or that are about to be planted up should be clean and free from weeds and the soil should be of a good, well cultivated condition and texture.

Good workmanship   **50 points**
Soil between the crops should contain little or no evidence of weeds. Paths and leisure areas where included should be neatly edged, even and well maintained. Evidence of planting for a constant succession of crops should be given credit. Intelligent use of organic methods of pest control such as the pinching out of broad bean tips to inhibit blackfly or the use of barriers against carrot root fly should be given credit. Supports for those plants that require them should be properly positioned and sturdy enough to withstand bad weather.

**Quality of crops, flowers, fruit and
vegetables and plants**   **150 points**
All plants should be vigorous, sturdy and free from obvious signs of excessive damage by pests, disease or weather. A broad range of food crops, both vegetables and fruit where the latter is permitted, should be in cultivation and flowers grown for cutting or decoration should be assessed on the same basis as the food crops ie with a regard to their health, skill in cultivation and suitability to the site. The inclusion of culinary herbs in the cropping scheme should be considered meritorious.

Originality of layout and planting   **25 points**
The intelligent adaptation of the layout to suit the needs of the plot-holder, the use of companion planting to reduce damage by pests and a pleasing overall visual effect should be considered meritorious. The cultivation of less common crops and the use of no-dig or deep-bed methods of cultivation should be given credit.

Ingenuity in overcoming local problems   **25 points**
Plot-holders who have overcome difficulties such as oddly shaped sites, difficult soil conditions, exposed aspect or excessive shading and dehydration by an adjacent tree belt

should be given credit for raising an acceptable (*ie* usable) standard of crop.

Visual aspect of the plot **20 points**

The overall appearance of the plot should be neat and pleasing and the balance of the cultivation, as far as is allowed by local regulations, should be as broad as possible.

Condition of garden sheds, etc **20 points**

Sheds, if present, should be of a neat and workmanlike appearance both inside and out. Frames, cloches and greenhouses should be clean and well maintained. Pea and bean supports should be sturdy enough for the weight of the crops that they bear and any bird netting should be properly positioned and undamaged so as to afford protection to the crops over which they have been placed.

TOTAL **350 points**

THE JUDGING OF
HANGING BASKETS AND
OTHER OUTDOOR
PLANTED CONTAINERS

The primary purpose of most hanging baskets, windowboxes and tubs is to decorate and improve the appearance of areas or structures that otherwise have little or no plant interest. Alternatively they may extend and complement the planted area of a garden.

Hanging baskets are usually for summer use only but windowboxes and tubs may be replanted several times during the year and may contain one or two bold-foliaged semi-permanent shrubs as basic structure planting.

In competition most credit should be given to bright bold colourful displays that succeed in catching the eye without being brash or vulgar.

Plants should be closely grouped and overflow the edges of their container so as to hide or almost hide it. They should be arranged in an attractive, well-balanced fashion and must be healthy and well developed with no obvious signs of damage by weather, pests or disease.

The planting should be selected and maintained to ensure an attractive display from early summer to the first autumn frost, unless otherwise specified by the competition schedule.

The flowers and foliage should be harmoniously co-ordinated to blend with each other and their setting. The use of a single colour or one single type of plant *eg* fuchsias or begonias, must not be considered a demerit provided the plants are well grown and attractively presented. Containers that use or include fruits or vegetables such as alpine strawberries, cherry tomatoes or non-hearting lettuce should be assessed on the same basis as those using flowering or foliage plants. Credit should be given as much for the appropriateness and decorative value of the plants as for their usefulness in providing fresh produce for the kitchen.

For those who require one, a pointing system is suggested as follows:

Initial impact of colours, and/or textures, and/or scent	50 points
Presentation, balance and symmetry of display	50 points
Quality, health, vigour and appropriateness of planting	70 points
Potential for long-term display	30 points
TOTAL	**200 points**

GLOSSARY

Alpine   Loosely applied to any plant that is suitable for a rock garden or alpine house.

Amateur   A person who, not being a professional either personally or with unpaid or paid assistance, maintains a garden or grows plants, flowers, fruit or vegetables for pleasure and enjoyment and not for a livelihood. (It is permissible for an amateur to sell surplus fruit and/or vegetables and/or other horticultural produce, provided that the garden is maintained primarily for the pleasure and enjoyment of the household and not as a means of livelihood.)

Annual   A plant that grows from seed and naturally and ordinarily flowers, seeds and dies (irrespective of frost) within twelve months.

Barrel   The shaft or stem of a leek.

Beard   The beard-like growth on the falls of some irises.

Biennial   A plant that grows from seed and ordinarily requires two seasons to complete its life-cycle, growing one year, flowering, seeding and dying in the second.

Blanch   That part of a leek stem which is blanched. In addition, that part of any vegetable that is blanched (*eg* celery, endive.)

Blemish   Mark or imperfection on exhibit that may be caused by mechanical damage, physiological deficiency, pest or disease.

Bloom   **1** The waxy covering of many fruits and vegetables, *eg* of a plum and a grape, and of the leaves and stems of many succulent and other plants. **2** A bloom: one open flower, *eg* of a tulip, or one flowerhead, *eg* of a chrysanthemum or dahlia *(see also **Flowerhead**, **Spike** and **Spray**)*. **3** In bloom: bearing at least one open flower. *(See p18, paragraph 14.)*

Bowl   A vessel for displaying cut flowers in water or for growing bulbous plants and having a mouth-width measurement at least equal to, but usually greater than, its height. In floral arrangement classes, bowls with one or more than one handle are acceptable.

Bract   Usually a small leaf-like structure occurring below the flowers and above the true leaves, but sometimes large and coloured, as in *Euphorbia*.

Bulb   An underground modified stem bearing a number of swollen fleshy leaf bases or scale leaves in which food is stored, the whole enclosing the next year's bud, *eg* the bulb of a daffodil, tulip, hyacinth or onion.

Bulbous   For horticultural-show purposes "bulbous plants" includes those having bulbs, corms or tubers; "bulbous" may also refer to a defective attribute such as the swelling of a plant, for example, the base of a leek.

Button   The point on the barrel of a leek where the lowest leaf breaks the circumference.

Cactus   A plant belonging to the family *Cactaceae*, *eg* species of *Cereus*, *Epiphyllum*, *Mammillaria*, *Opuntia* or *Schlumbergera*.

Calyx   The outer set of perianth segments, especially when green.

Challenge cup   A challenge cup or trophy is one that does not become the property of the winner at the first contest but is intended either for periodical (usually annual) contests in perpetuity or to become the property of a competitor only after he/she has won it on a specified number of occasions in accordance with the regulations for the particular cup or trophy.

Class   A sub-division of a competitive schedule; one group of comparable exhibits.

Collection   An assembly of kinds and/or cultivars of plants, flowers, fruits or vegetables in one exhibit.

Conifers   Members of the family *Coniferae*, which for show purposes includes maidenhair tree (*Ginkgo*).

Container   A general term, used particularly in connection with floral arrangements, for bowls, vases and other vessels used to display plants or flowers.

Corm   For horticultural-show purposes, a bulb-like swollen underground stem stored with reserve food, *eg Crocus*, *Colchicum* or *Gladiolus*.

Corolla   The inner set of perianth segments, if differing from the outer set, and especially if coloured and showy.

Corona   A trumpet- or cup-like development of the perianth found in *Narcissus* species and cultivars.

Cultivar   The internationally accepted term for what, in English-speaking countries, is commonly known by horticulturists as a "cultivated variety" or simply a "variety". *(See **Variety** for the distinction between a cultivar and a botanical variety.)*

Deciduous   A deciduous tree or shrub is one having leaves that persist only one season and fall in the autumn.

Dish   In horticultural-show schedules, a specified number or quantity of a fruit or vegetable constituting one item that may be displayed on a table or on a stand or on a receptacle of any material and of any shape. Unless specially permitted by the schedule, a dish must consist of one cultivar only.

Display An exhibit in which attractiveness of arrangement and general effect are to be considered of more importance than they would have been had the schedule specified a "group" or a "collection".

Disqualify To remove from the judges' consideration because of non-compliance with the specification in the schedule or with a rule governing the competition.

Entry A notification of an intention to exhibit; a unit submitted for exhibition in a competition or show.

Evergreen A plant that retains its living foliage for at least a full year and is never leafless.

Everlasting A plant with flowerheads that retain much of their showy character after being cut and dried.

Falls The three outer segments of an iris flower.

Flags The leaves of a leek plant.

Florets Small individual flowers, especially those in heads, as in a chrysanthemum, dahlia or other members of *Asteraceae*.

Flowerhead For horticultural-show purposes, an assemblage of florets grouped together in a single head on a single flower stem, *eg* a disbudded chrysanthemum or a disbudded dahlia.

Foliage 1 The leaves of any plant. 2 Stems bearing only leaves.

Foliage Plant A plant usually grown for its ornamental foliage. If they are in flower they may be entered into a foliage-plant class but the flowers will not be taken into account.

Forced Grown to flower or be ready for consumption before the normal time.

Frond A leaf of a fern or palm.

Fruits 1 In classes for edible fruits: "fruits" means those normally grown for dessert or for eating when cooked as pudding. 2 In classes for ornamental fruits and for floral arrangements: "fruits" means all types of developed ovaries, *eg* seed pods, berries and ornamental gourds.

Genus A group of related plants having the same generic name, *eg* all species and hybrids of the genus *Lilium*, such as *L. candidum*, *L. chalcedonicum*, *L.* 'Enchantment', *L. henryi*, *L. regale* and *L. × testaceum*.

Gourds, edible More usually described as winter squash. *See Squash.*

Gourds, ornamental   Edible and inedible fruits of the family *Cucurbitaceae*. Most are small, of various colours and colour patterns, smooth, warted or with other protuberances. Large specimens can have long necks, *eg* Swan or Dolphin. Used for ornament and in flower arranging, varnished or unvarnished, fresh or dried. Ornamental gourds cannot be shown in vegetable classes.

Grown in the open   1 In classes for fruit the expression means that the plants or trees have flowered and also set their fruit, as well as ripened it, without any protection beyond netting or a wall-coping not exceeding 600mm in width. 2 In classes for vegetables, for annuals, for plants grown as annuals and for half-hardy ornamental plants, the expression means that the plants have been grown in the ground in the open air without any protection by glass or glass substitute once the danger of spring frosts has passed. 3 In classes for hardy herbaceous plants, trees and shrubs the expression means those grown in the ground in the open air and not with protection by glass or glass substitutes.

Habit   The general appearance or manner of growth of a plant, *eg* compact, straggling, tufted, bushy, shrubby.

Half-hardy   A half-hardy plant is one that may be grown in the open air for part of the year but must be lifted and housed or protected in some other way during winter. In the case of an annual: one that may either be raised under glass and planted out when frosts are no longer feared or sown out of doors in May or early June.

Hardy   A hardy plant is one that is able to survive the average winter when grown in the open without protection.

Herb   For horticultural-show purposes a culinary "herb" is an essential ingredient in many foods, which makes it of value for flavouring soups, stews, sauces, salads, etc, the following being among the more important kinds: angelica, basil, bay, borage, celery leaf, chervil, chives, coriander, dill, fennel, hyssop, lemon balm, lovage, marjoram, mint, oregano, parsley, rocket, rosemary, sage (*S. officinalis* only), savory, sorrel, sweet cicely (*Myrrhis*), tarragon and thyme. Seed forms such as coriander and dill and root forms such as Florence fennel should not be included.

Herbaceous perennial   A plant with a non-woody stem that either dies down to the ground completely each winter, *eg* delphinium, or retains its basal foliage, *eg* bergenia, but which has a rootstock that remains alive throughout several years. For horticultural purposes the word "rootstock" includes all bulbs, corms, rhizomes and tubers unless specifically excluded by a show schedule.

Herbaceous plant A plant that does not form a persistent woody stem. It may be annual, biennial or perennial.

Hilum The scar on a seed marking the point of attachment to the plant.

House plant A plant grown for the decorative effect of its foliage, flower or fruit and which, given reasonable treatment, will thrive in a dwelling room for several years. *See pp135–137.*

Hybrid A plant derived from the intercrossing of two or more genetically distinct plants (in ornamental horticulture, usually two or more species), *eg Lilium × testaceum* is a hybrid resulting from the interbreeding of *L. candidum* and *L. chalcedonicum*; *×Brassocattleya holfordii* is a hybrid resulting from the intercrossing of *Brassavola digbyana* and *Cattleya forbesii*. F_1 hybrids of vegetables and seed-raised flowers are plants raised from seed obtained from crosses between selected parent lines, which themselves can be maintained in the same state over many generations so the hybridization can be repeated many times over a period of years.

Inflorescence The flowering portion of the stem above the last stem leaves, including its flower branches, bracts and flowers.

Kind 1 A term recommended for use in the classification of fruit and vegetables for show purposes, *eg* apples, grapes, peaches, pears and plums are "kinds" of fruit; asparagus, carrots, onions and peas are "kinds" of vegetable. *Refer to p49 and pp70–72 for lists of different kinds of fruit and vegetables.*
2 When applied to ornamental flowers, the term kind is botanically incorrect but has become accepted for show purposes to differentiate between genera. However, the term also applies to annual and perennial forms within the same genera, *eg* annual asters and Michaelmas daisies.
3 Technically, there is no real way in which this type of categorisation can be properly applied to ornamental plants such as annuals, herbaceous plants, trees and shrubs, etc. These plants are all, broadly speaking, either species or cultivars and those with common characteristics are gathered together in groups called genera which in turn are grouped in families. Thus *Iris danfordiae* and the tall bearded *Iris* 'Grace' are a species and a cultivar of the genus *Iris* which in turn is one of the genera of the family *Iridaceae*. For show purposes, where the object is to attract a wide diversity of plants into a collection class, it is best to word the schedule to invite "Six hardy herbaceous plants representing at least three genera, one vase of each" or "Four species or cultivars of bulbous plants

representing two or more genera, one vase of each" or similar adaptations of these wordings.

Leeks   For exhibition purposes leeks are divided into three categories: **1 Pot:** not more than 150mm from base to button. **2 Intermediate:** not less than 150mm and not more than 350mm from base to button. **3 Blanched:** more than 350mm from base to button.

Marrow   A nearly full-sized but immature fruit of *Cucurbita pepo*. The skin should be tender. The shape should be cylindrical with blunt ends; traditionally with green stripes but may be other colours.

Natural   "Natural", as applied to foliage, flowers or fruits, means as produced by the plant, without any artificial treatment such as dyeing, oiling or varnishing.

Novice   A competitor who has not won at a previous show some prize or prizes specified in the definition of a novice in the schedule.

Originality   In a schedule "originality" means uncommon or unusual but at the same time desirable.

Panicle   For horticultural-show purposes, a branched inflorescence.

Pedicel   The stalk of a single flower on an inflorescence *(see Peduncle)*.

Peduncle   The stalk of an inflorescence or of part of an inflorescence. This term should also be used for a stalk of an inflorescence with a solitary flower *(See also Pedicel)*.

Perennial   A perennial plant is one that lives for more than two years. Perennial plants include trees and shrubs, plants that grow from bulbs, corms, rhizomes and tubers and, in fact, all that are not annuals or biennials. (Antirrhinums, petunias, wallflowers and some other plants are usually grown as annuals or biennials in gardens but, botanically, may be true perennials. In such cases, it is recommended that the horticultural practice of treating them as annuals should be adopted for show purposes to avoid confusion.) *(See p24, paragraph 18.)*

Perianth   A term used for the calyx and corolla or their equivalents but seldom used except when the segments of the two whorls are both coloured, as in a daffodil or a tulip.

Petal   An individual segment of the corolla, especially one free to the base.

Pip   **1** An individual flower of an inflorescence, applied especially to auriculas, delphiniums, gladioli and sweet williams. **2** A bulbil within the inflorescence of leeks, onions and other alliums. **3** The seed within a fruit such as apple or pear.

Pot plant   For horticultural-show purposes, a plant grown in a pot for the decorative effect of its foliage, flower or fruit and for use in a glasshouse or, for a short period, in a dwelling room. *See pp135–137.*

Professional   A person who gains his/her livelihood by growing horticultural plants, flowers, fruit or vegetables for sale or for an employer or anyone employed in the maintenance of a garden, pleasure ground or park.

Pumpkins   Traditionally these are mature fruits ripening to orange and with a hollow seed cavity used for carving into Halloween faces. Principally *Cucurbita pepo* but some large specimens are *C. maxima*, such as 'Mammoth Gourd', 'Mammoth Gold', 'Atlantic Giant', 'Sumo' and 'Prizewinner'. *(See also Squash)*

Radish, Oriental and winter   Usually large, round or long-pointed roots, which can weigh up to 2kg in the case of Oriental radishes and up to 1kg for winter radishes. Long white Oriental radishes, known as moolis, and coloured-skinned cultivars with red, white or green flesh are included in this category.

Radish, small salad   Quick growing, tender rooted, round to oval with a diameter of approximately 30mm, coloured red, white, occasionally yellow, or red with white lower half. French Breakfast types with roots about 75mm long, blunt-ended with white tip of varying proportions. Also white, pointed roots up to 100mm long.

Ray-florets   The outer florets of a flowerhead, such as that of a daisy, often larger than the inner florets.

Rhizome   An underground, usually horizontal, swollen stem containing food reserves, *eg* bearded irises.

Rhubarb   Although commonly eaten as a dessert this plant is classified as a vegetable for all show purposes.

Root vegetable   For horticultural-show purposes, root vegetables include the following kinds: artichokes (Chinese and Jerusalem), beetroot, carrots, celeriac, kohlrabi, parsnips, potatoes, radishes, salsify, scorzonera, swedes and turnips.

Rootstock or stock   **1** In the context of fruit, refers to the plant on to which the fruit-bearing material has been grafted or budded. **2** It also applies to the stocks used in the grafting or budding of ornamental plants.

Rose end   The end of a potato tuber where the dormant buds, or "eyes", are concentrated.

Salading or salad vegetable   A vegetable used in either a raw or cooked state and served in salads as a cold dish. The following examples are kinds that may be used for horticultural-show purposes: beetroot, cabbages, carrots, celeriac, celery, chicory, chives, corn salad or lambs' lettuce, cress, cress (American or land), cucumbers, dandelion (blanched), endive, Florence fennel, kohlrabi, lettuces, mustard or rape, onions (green salad), oriental brassicas, potatoes, radishes, sweet peppers, tomatoes, turnips and watercress.

Scape   A long, naked or nearly naked peduncle, whether one- or many-flowered, rising directly from the base of a plant.

Seedling   1 A young plant that has recently germinated. 2 A plant of any age raised from seed as opposed to one propagated by grafting or other vegetative means. 3 For horticultural-show purposes a distinct new cultivar (variety) raised from seed and not yet named.

Sepal   An individual segment of the calyx.

Shrub   A woody perennial, often many-stemmed, of smaller structure than a tree and having no distinct bole or trunk.

Soft fruit   A fruit having a soft texture and numerous seeds, *eg* a blackberry, currant, gooseberry, loganberry, raspberry or strawberry.

Species   A group of closely related plants of one genus having the same specific name; *eg Lilium candidum*, *L. henryi*, *L. martagon* and *L. regale* are four species of *Lilium*; *L. martagon* var. *cattaniæ* and *L. martagon* var. *hirsutum* are both botanical varieties of one species, *Lilium martagon*.

Spike   For horticultural-show purposes, a spike is an unbranched (or only very slightly branched) inflorescence with an elongated axis, bearing either stalked or stalkless flowers, as in a cymbidium, delphinium, foxglove, gladiolus, hollyhock or odontoglossum.

Sport   A sport from a particular cultivar (variety) is a plant propagated vegetatively from a mutated part of the parent cultivar (variety).

Spray   For horticultural-show purposes, a spray is a branched, many-flowered inflorescence usually on a single main stem.

Squash   American terminology for fruits of the genus *Cucurbita*. There are two types: summer squash and winter squash. Summer squash are fruit eaten and shown at the immature stage, and include scallops or patty pans, custard marrows, crooknecks, mostly of species *C. pepo*. (Courgettes and marrows could be, but are not, considered in this class.) Winter squash are generally those cultivars whose fruits are eaten at the fully mature stage, and which can be stored for winter use. They are generally of the species *C. maxima* and *C. moschata* but also some *C. pepo*. Cultivars of winter squash include 'Acorn', 'Buttercup', 'Butternut', 'Crown Prince', 'Hubbard's', 'Kabocha', 'Onion Squash', 'Sweet Dumpling', 'Turk's Turban' and 'Vegetable Spaghetti'.

Standard 1 A term that, when applied to a tree or other plant, means a specimen with an upright stem of some length supporting a head, *eg* the standard is a common form for "permanent" orchard trees of apples, pears and plums. Roses, fuchsias, heliotropes and chrysanthemums are some ornamental plants readily grown as standards. 2 When applied to a sweet pea or other papilionaceous flowers it describes the, usually upright, back petal of the corolla. 3 When applied to an iris it describes one of the three inner perianth segments.

Stone fruit A fruit with a soft, fleshy interior, surrounding a comparatively large "stone" containing, usually, a solitary seed, *eg* an apricot, cherry, damson, peach or plum.

Strig A term relating to currants and to berries of a similar bearing habit such as jostaberry, worcesterberry and blueberry. Strig indicates a bunch or, in botanical terms, a complete raceme or panicle of berries. It is best detached from the plant with scissors and should not include any of the woody section at the base.

Succulent A plant with very fleshy leaves or stems or both, *eg* species of *Cotyledon*, *Crassula*, *Echeveria*, *Hoya*, *Kalanchoe*, *Sedum*, *Sempervivum* and most *Cactaceae*.

Tender A tender plant is one that requires a favourable locality or situation and that, under severe climatic conditions, may need some form of protection during winter.

Tree A perennial woody plant with an evident bole or trunk, but sometimes multi-stemmed.

Truss A cluster of flowers or fruits growing from one main stem, as in a pelargonium, polyanthus, rhododendron or tomato.

Tuber A swollen underground stem with buds or "eyes" from which new plants or tubers are produced, *eg* Jerusalem artichoke, tuberous begonia, dahlia, gloriosa, gloxinia, potato and runner bean.

Uniformity   The state of being alike in size, shape, condition and colour.

Variety   In scientific usage the term "variety" (*varietas*) is a botanical category restricted to a naturally occurring variant of a species; "botanical varieties" are given Latin names, preceded by the abbreviation var. and begin with a small letter (*eg Paeonia lutea* var. *ludlowii*). Variants of species and hybrids produced by man in cultivation are termed cultivars and are given non-Latin "fancy" names, though some old cultivars, which have had Latin names for many years, retain these names; cultivar names begin with a capital letter and follow directly after the Latin or English name of the species or hybrid concerned, enclosed in single quotation marks (*eg Syringa vulgaris* 'Mont Blanc'; *Dahlia* 'Hamari Sunshine''; *Juniperus procumbens* 'Nana'; *Viburnum* × *bodnantense* 'Dawn'). In English-speaking countries horticulturists have long used the word "variety" to cover both "botanical variety" and "cultivar", but as the term "cultivar" is now becoming increasingly accepted, it is recommended that it should be used in show schedules when appropriate.

Vase   A vessel for displaying cut flowers in water and having a greater height than the width-measurement of its mouth. Unless otherwise required or permitted by the schedule a vase may contain only one cultivar (variety). In floral arrangement classes, vases with one or more than one handle are acceptable. Where standard vases are not provided by show organisers, judges should exercise discretion in regarding as eligible any container that fulfils the function of a vase and conforms to the definition given above, provided that no account is taken of the container when judging the material shown in it.

Vegetable   For horticultural-show purposes, a vegetable is a plant (or part of a plant) normally grown in the kitchen garden to be eaten either cooked or less often raw but not usually as dessert or as a pudding. Rhubarb, though commonly eaten as dessert, is classified as a vegetable. Aubergines, beans, courgettes, cucumbers, marrows, mushrooms, okra, peppers, peas, pumpkins, squash, sweet corn and tomatoes, though botanically fruits, are here classified as vegetables.

Veil   In leeks, a thin white transparent skin that is present across and above the button where the leaf opens out from the sheath and which is included in the measurements.

INDEX

P

pak choi 93
panicle, definition 160
pansies:
    fancy (exhibition
      cultivars) 132
    fancy (garden cultivars)
      133
    show 132–133
parsley 40
    see also herbs
parsnips 40, 72, 73, 94
passion fruits 49, 50, 63
peaches 34, 35, 49, 50, 59
pears 24, 34, 35, 36, 49
    Asian 49, 50, 60
    classified list 68
    cooking 50, 60
    dessert 50, 60
peas 40, 72, 73, 94, 164
    asparagus 37, 70, 73, 75
    mangetout 37, 73, 95
    snap 37, 73, 95
pedicel, definition 160
peduncle, definition 160
pelargoniums:
    ivy-leaved 133
    regal 134
    zonal 134
peppers:
    hot (chilli) 40, 72, 73, 95,
      164
    sweet 40, 72, 73, 95, 164
perennials:
    classes 24
    definition 160
perianth, definition 160
persimmons 49, 50, 63
pest infestations 46
petal, definition 160
pineapple guavas 49, 50, 63
pineapples 49, 50, 61
pinks 134–135
pip, definition 160–161

plums 34, 36, 49
    classified list 69
    cooking 50, 61, 69
    dessert 50, 61, 69
points:
    maximum for fruits 50
    maximum for vegetables
      73–74
polyanthus 135
pot plants 135–137
    definition 161
potatoes 40, 72, 73, 95
    classes for 25, 26–27
pots, size 26
primroses 137
Primula species 138
prize cards 14–15
prizes:
    not everything 29
    one per class 11
    point-value 22
    relative value 22
    withholding 11, 15, 18,
      22–23
prizewinners, recording 17
professional gardeners:
    definition 161
    exhibits from 13
protests 12, 19, 31
pumpkins 40, 72, 73, 96, 164
    definition 161

Q

quinces 35, 36, 49, 50, 62

Notes